W9-BGZ-191

THE MULTIPLE INTELLIGENCES HANDBOOK

Lesson Plans and More...

Bruce Campbell

Campbell & Associates

© 1994 BY BRUCE CAMPBELL

ALL RIGHTS RESERVED. NO PART OF THIS PUBLICATION MAY BE REPRODUCED
OR TRANSMITTED IN ANY FORM BY ANY MEANS, ELECTRONIC OR MECHANICAL,
INCLUDING PHOTOCOPY, RECORDING, OR ANY INFORMATION STORAGE AND
RETRIEVAL SYSTEM, WITHOUT PERMISSION IN WRITING FROM THE AUTHOR.

Editing: Linda Campbell
Dorothy Bestor

Design: Jean C. Lilley

ISBN 0-96420 37-0-7

Permission is granted to copy forms in this book for classroom use.

CAMPBELL & ASSOC., INC.
17410 Marine Drive
Stanwood, WA 98292
Fax (360) 652-9503

To Linda Campbell and Howard Gardner, I extend my deepest thanks.

I thank Linda, my wife, for her wealth of ideas, extensive editing, and endless support.

I thank Dr. Gardner for his ongoing inspiration and encouragement. With his Theory of Multiple Intelligences, he has articulated what many teachers intuitively know - that each child is gifted. In so doing, he has provided us with a framework for revisioning education.

I also thank my students at Cascade Elementary School in Marysville, Washington who eagerly embraced our Multiple Intelligences class-room and helped to develop and refine many of the units, activities, and processes included in this book.

This book is dedicated to
each teacher who tries to instill
a love of learning in each child.

TABLE OF CONTENTS

Introduction:

Welcome to the MI Handbook! This handbook has emerged from my years of teaching through the Multiple Intelligences in an elementary, multi-age classroom. I wrote this book to share with other teachers what I have learned. I will begin with a story about one of my students named Richard and then briefly introduce Howard Gardner's Theory of Multiple Intelligences.

RICHARD'S BREAKTHROUGH

"Mr. Campbell! Mr. Campbell! Come over to the Ray Charles Center and listen to what Richard taught us. "

"Okay, just a second."

"No—this is really good! You have to come right now!"

I let Kristina finish the paragraph she was reading to me and moved to the classroom music center. A group of four students—two fifth graders, a fourth grader, and Richard, a third grader—were working with a small keyboard and hand-made percussion instruments on what we called a two-part rhythm.

At the time, we were studying cells, the building blocks of life, and the way many cells in the body divide at the same time. To develop this concept musically, the students at the Ray Charles Center were creating rhythmic accompaniment to lyrics about mitosis.

As I arrived, the group explained that Richard had taught them to play an intricate three-part rhythm. This lively and inviting composition was completely of the group's creation. Soon, the whole class (not easily distracted, since students are used to lots of daily activity) had gathered around. The piece went on for about four minutes. The class stood in awe. No group had composed such complex music and this was clearly beyond anything I had suggested or demonstrated. In fact, it was well beyond anything I knew how to do.

As the composition reached a crescendo and ended with a natural cadence, the class spontaneously erupted in applause. They all recognized good music created right in their own classroom.

Most remarkable was Richard's role in the development of the composition. Richard had difficulty in nearly all subject areas—he had been identified for pull-out programs and labelled a special education student. What was surprising about his role as primary composer at the Ray Charles Center was that nobody, including Richard, himself, had known he was musically proficient. What we witnessed was the sudden unfolding of a unique musical talent.

Richard had had no musical training at home or at school other than his daily work at the Ray Charles Center. After five months of working with music in the classroom, Richard discovered an inherent talent. His classmates, duly impressed, congratulated him. Their praise was a new experience for someone who had rarely been successful.

Over the next few days, Richard's musical accomplishments continued. Soon students from other classes were coming to listen. Interestingly, Richard himself began to change—he carried himself with more pride, and he began taking academic risks that he would have previously avoided.

By the end of the school year, Richard had grown in many ways. I ran into him one day in the middle of the summer vacation. He was exuberant as he told me he had his own keyboard and was "making music like mad." This was not the same reticent, withdrawn, third grader I had met just ten months earlier.

Richard's story might be more dramatic than some, but it's not unusual in a Multiple Intelligences classroom. When students learn in diverse ways on a daily basis, they frequently experience breakthroughs. Such breakthroughs include identifying areas of strength, using strengths to overcome weaknesses, discovering a love of learning, and even scoring well on standardized tests!

This book was written to assist teachers who are interested in working with the Multiple Intelligences in their classrooms. It is based on my seven years of experience teaching through the Multiple Intelligences. This book is written as a direct response to the teachers who have asked me "How do we start?" "What resources do we need?" And most commonly, "Do you have MI lesson plans to share?"

The MI Handbook, while certainly not everything you ever needed to know about the Multiple Intelligences, is a useful tool to help you with your efforts to teach to the strengths of each student. Good luck!

Bruce Campbell

Getting Acquainted with Multiple Intelligences

Before explaining what I have learned about teaching through the Multiple Intelligences, I think it is important to acknowledge the source of inspiration for my efforts. Howard Gardner is a cognitive psychologist at Harvard University. In 1983, his book *Frames of Mind: The Theory of Multiple Intelligences* was published. His work expanded the traditional notion of intelligence beyond linguistic and mathematical competencies and redefined what intelligence is. According to Gardner, human intelligence consists of three components:

♦ *a set of skills that enables an individual to resolve genuine*
  problems encountered in one's life;

♦ *the ability to create an effective product or offer a service*
  that is of value in one's culture; and

♦ *the potential for finding or creating problems which enables*
  an individual to acquire new knowledge.

To arrive at this enhanced view of intelligence, Gardner studied the cognitive profiles of gifted children, people from diverse cultures, idiots savants, and brain-damaged individuals. He realized that intelligence was expressed in multiple forms—in addition to linguistic and logical-mathematical abilities, he identified kinesthetic, visual-spatial, musical, interpersonal, and intrapersonal intelligences. The seven identified intelligences are as follows:

 **Linguistic intelligence** is the ability to think in words and to use language to express and appreciate complex meanings. Linguistic intelligence allows us to understand the order and meaning of words, and to apply metalinguistic skills to reflect on our use of language. Linguistic intelligence is the most widely shared human competence and is evident in poets, novelists, journalists, and effective public speakers.

 Logical-mathematical intelligence is the ability to calculate, quantify, consider propositions and hypotheses, and carry out complex mathematical operations. It enables us to perceive relationships and connections, to use abstract, symbolic thought, sequential reasoning skills, and inductive and deductive thinking processes. Logical intelligence is usually well-developed in mathematicians, scientists, and detectives.

Bodily-kinesthetic intelligence is the capacity to manipulate objects and use a variety of physical skills. This intelligence also involves a sense of timing, and the perfection of skills through mind-body union. Athletes, dancers, surgeons, and craftspeople exhibit highly developed kinesthetic intelligence.

Spatial intelligence is the ability to think in three dimensions. Core capacities of this intelligence include mental imagery, spatial reasoning, image manipulation, graphic and artistic skills, and an active imagination. Sailors, pilots, sculptors, painters, and architects all exhibit spatial intelligence.

Musical intelligence is the capacity to discern pitch, rhythm, timbre, and tone. This intelligence enables one to recognize, create, reproduce, and reflect on music, as demonstrated by composers, conductors, musicians, vocalists, and sensitive listeners. Interestingly, there is often an affective connection between music and the emotions, and mathematical and musical intelligences may share common thinking processes.

Interpersonal intelligence is the ability to understand and interact effectively with others It involves effective verbal and non-verbal communication, the ability to note distinctions among others, a sensitivity to the moods and temperaments of others, and the ability to entertain multiple perspectives. Teachers, social workers, actors, and politicians all exhibit interpersonal intelligence.

Intrapersonal intelligence is the capacity to understand oneself — one's thoughts and feelings and to use such knowledge in planning and directing one's life. Intrapersonal intelligence involves not only an appreciation of the self, but also of the human condition and is evident in psychologists, spiritual leaders, and philosophers.

The implications of Gardner's work for education are extensive. If we accept the idea that individuals have diverse cognitive profiles, then pedagogy, curriculum, and assessment will need to change so that students can learn and demonstrate their learning in different ways. Students deserve opportunities to work from their strengths, to enhance their areas of weakness, and to discover what they most enjoy and love to do. The rest of this book is dedicated to nurturing the gifts in each child.

PART I:
PREPARING THE
MI CLASSROOM

Part 1 answers the question: How do you start a Multiple Intelligences program?

In this section, you will find descriptions of several existing Multiple Intelligences classrooms so that you can identify a variety of ways to infuse MI into your classroom. I next describe my own classroom, which has been in place since 1987 and which has been replicated successfully in hundreds of other classrooms around the United States. Since teachers often request additional information on the seven learning centers in my classroom, I explain how they were named, and how I group students for center work. Part I closes with suggesting steps to start a MI program, and by identifying some of the resources to gather. This initial section includes:

Diverse Multiple Intelligences Classroom Models

Daily Format in one MI Classroom

Multiple Intelligences Centers

Grouping Students for MI Centers or Cooperative Learning

Starting a Multiple Intelligences Program

Resources for an MI Classroom

Diverse Multiple Intelligences Classroom Models

There are as many ways to set up an MI classroom as there are teachers — each teacher must determine what is most appropriate for his/her teaching approach, grade level, subject area, and students. To assist teachers in planning an MI classroom, several models of actual K-12 MI programs are listed below. Some models focus on learning centers, others use traditional, direct instruction approaches. Although many teachers assume that a centers-based approach works best at the elementary level, a few secondary teachers are finding great success with this format as well. All the MI models can be used with single-subject, interdisciplinary, or thematic instruction. Teachers may want to read through the MI classroom models to identify ones that seem appropriate for their classrooms or to use them as a source of inspiration for creating additional MI approaches.

Seven learning centers each day:

This model features seven learning centers, each dedicated to one of Gardner's intelligences. The curriculum is thematic and interdisciplinary—students move through the centers learning about the topic in seven ways. One advantage of this model is that it keeps group size small.

Three to five learning centers each day:

This model is similar to the one above. Often the two personal intelligences are eliminated since they are incorporated into activities at other centers. Another variation is to have the intelligence centers change from day to day or week to week: for example, music and movement would rotate. This model provides flexibility for the teacher and multiple options for students.

Learning centers once weekly:

In this model, five to seven centers are set up but only on one or two days per week. A special topic would be studied on these days, with a return to a traditional classroom format during the rest of the week. This method involves more set-up/take-down time, but it is an excellent way for teachers to experiment with MI.

Whole class moves together to different classrooms:

This is an interesting elementary model based on team-teaching. The teachers remain in separate classrooms with students moving as a whole class from room to room every 40 to 60 minutes. The curriculum is interdisciplinary, with students learning about the topic from two or more teachers. Teachers serve as "intelligence experts" and co-plan their units, with each contributing from one or more areas of individual strength. What distinguishes this model from traditional secondary schools is that the students move together as a single cohort from room to room.

Whole-class instruction in multiple ways:

This model features a traditional classroom environment with direct instruction, however, learning activities regularly include musical, kinesthetic, visual, interpersonal, and intrapersonal techniques. This model is probably the easiest way for teachers to begin working with the Multiple Intelligences.

One intelligence is emphasized:

This model is another variation of the whole-class approach—the teacher highlights one intelligence per day. For example, on a Monday, the teacher might ask students to work together in a variety of cooperative learning strategies to engage interpersonal intelligence. On Tuesday, they might graph or draw the content of their lessons to learn visually. Over the course of seven school days, each student would have opportunities to learn through all seven intelligences. Some teachers include an eighth day in the cycle—on this day students have free choice to learn however they prefer.

Self-directed learning—students' choice based upon individual strengths:

In this approach, students have opportunities to pursue projects of their choice. Students plan their learning activities, frequently using Student Learning Contracts (see sample contract in the independent projects section). They set goals, create timelines, conduct independent research, and determine how to demonstrate their learning. The teacher serves as a facilitator and resource person. This approach can be used occasionally—such as twice quarterly at the secondary level—or it can be a regular feature of each elementary school day.

Apprenticeship programs:

There are numerous apprenticeship options that assist students in developing in-depth skills. Individual teachers can ask parent or community volunteers to share their expertise with small groups of students. For example, on Tuesdays, three community members—a journalist, a pianist, and an actor—might work with students interested in their specialties. Some schoolwide apprenticeship programs feature once-weekly options for the entire student body. If an individual teacher or an entire school is interested in apprenticeships, it is important to structure them so that they span several months at a time. In this way, students develop extensive knowledge and skills in a particular intelligence area.

Daily Format in One MI Classroom Using Seven Learning Centers

Since 1987, I have implemented an MI classroom model that includes seven learning centers and a thematic, integrated curriculum. Each center is dedicated to one of the seven intelligences. During the morning, students learn about the day's topic at several centers. In the afternoon, they work on self-selected projects and apply their diverse learning skills to areas of individual interest. This classroom model works well for me, but it is certainly not the only effective MI approach. Again, I think it is vitally important for each teacher to discover how best to work with Gardner's ideas. The description below of how I conduct my classroom is offered as a glimpse into one MI program's daily schedule.

Opening:

After the morning's attendance and announcements, I lead the students in a quick discussion. This "warm-up" typically involves a news event, a current student or school problem, or a controversial social issue. Students are challenged to form opinions, question each other's points of view, and substantiate their own statements. The discussion is brief and lively.

Main Lesson:

After our morning warm-up, I teach what I call my "main lesson." Students are required to take notes in their journals on each day's main lesson. The lesson consists of a 10 to 15 minute overview of one aspect of the theme the class is studying. For example, in a unit about outer space, the morning lesson might be on comets and what causes their elongated orbits. The lesson usually includes visuals and sometimes hands-on activities. Occasionally , it is taught by a student who has volunteered, a parent with some expertise, or somone from the community with interest in the topic. The main lesson sets a context for the activities that follow in the seven learning centers.

Directions:

I then give directions for the activities at each of the learning centers. Since some of the center activities are usually continued from the previous day, only three or four directions may be given.

Center Work:

For the next two hours, students move in small groups through the seven learning centers. Each group spends about 25 to 30 minutes at each center before rotating to the next. Center work involves learning about the main lesson in seven different ways. For example, at the music center students learn through singing or composing. It takes two days for the class to move through all seven centers. Usually four centers are completed on the first day and the other three on the second.

The centers provide time for both collaborative and independent learning. Textbooks are integrated into center activities when their content matches the lesson. The centers offer students opportunities to learn content as well as to develop diverse thinking and learning skills.

Some teachers might look at seven centers and see a great amount of planning. But the planning is minimized by two factors: first, we begin new centers only twice a week — on Mondays and Wednesdays since it takes the groups two days to rotate through all seven centers; second, many of the activities are continued for several days or even weeks. On Friday, we have "free centers" which the students often plan themselves and which provide opportunities to complete unfinished work from earlier in the week.

Sharing:

After working at the centers, students gather as a whole group to share their learning and to receive feedback from their peers. Only those students who volunteer sing their songs, perform their skits, read their written work, or show their art products to the rest of the class. Students offer compliments and constructive criticism to one another. Daily sharing typically requires from five to twenty minutes and concludes the first half of the school day.

Math:

The afternoon begins with a math lesson I teach to the whole class. For my math instruction, I use a combination of manipulatives to teach concepts as well as drill and practice activities. The math lesson is usually 45 minutes long and is enriched by activities in the Math Center on subsequent mornings.

Projects:

Next, students work on their independent projects for approximately one hour daily. Students choose their own topics and pursue them individually or in pairs. Project work is organized with a contract that specifies what students will accomplish when. Students are expected to become "junior experts" and to teach others what they have learned. They identify their topics, research them, and prepare a multimodal presentation for the rest of the class. Each project usually requires three to four weeks of preparation. When students share their projects with the rest of the class, their presentations reveal the learning skills they have gained at the seven centers, as well as the knowledge they have acquired from their research. The presentations also demonstrate that students can identify their interests, set goals, and achieve them in self-directed ways.

Review:

At the end of the day, I conduct a short review of our main lesson, the seven centers, and project efforts. I may also assign homework during the review, as well as preview the next day's main lesson. For example, I might say, "Today, we learned about comets and their strange orbits around the sun. What are other objects that orbit the sun?... Tomorrow's lesson is on asteroids." The preview serves as a bridge connecting today's lesson with tomorrow's. It also weaves together the unit and the theme.

Multiple Intelligences Centers

Initially, when I began teaching through seven learning centers, I identified each with a name that emphasized its function. For example, for kinesthetic intelligence, the center was named The Building Center. The visual center was called The Art Center, and so on. At the start of the second year of my program a student teacher suggested that the centers be named after famous people who exhibited each of the seven intelligences. Together we brainstormed whom the centers might feature and generated a list of exemplary individuals. I have named the centers after famous individuals every year since, and it is an idea that has caught on with many educators around the country.

Highlighting intelligence experts at the centers offers numerous curricular possibilities. My students spend the first week of school learning about the Multiple Intelligences and seven talented individuals. After learning about such people, how they developed their skills, and the kinds of social contributions they made, the students begin to expect that their own capacities will develop over time and that they may, too, make wonderful contributions. Another phenomenon I have observed is that students begin to identify with certain individuals. It is almost as if the seven geniuses begin to serve as "mentors in absentia" for my students. Also, when an individual student exhibits particularly strong skills her classmates may refer to her as the class's Picasso or Emily Dickinson.

I change the names of some of my centers each year. For example, the kinesthetic center has changed from Thomas Edison to Martha Graham. When the center was named for Thomas Edison, I provided a variety of building and inventing activities. With the change to Martha Graham, I emphasize creative movement and dance. The center names actually guide my curriculum planning throughout the course of a year. My centers are currently dedicated to the following people:

MI Center Names

William Shakespeare Center	Linguistic Intelligence
Albert Einstein Center	Logical-Mathematical Intelligence
Martha Graham Center	Kinesthetic Intelligence
Pablo Picasso Center	Visual-Spatial Intelligence
Ray Charles Center	Musical Intelligence
Mother Teresa Center	Interpersonal Intelligence
Emily Dickinson Center	Intrapersonal Intelligence

Numerous teachers have experimented with ways to name their centers. One teacher named the centers after teachers in her building, another after seven famous women, a third after fictional characters, and another after members of the community who then served as classroom mentors by regularly visiting the school and sharing their expertise with students. Some teachers change center names during the year, while others encourage their students to choose center names on a quarterly basis.

Grouping Students for MI Centers or Cooperative Learning

I am often asked how I group my students for their work at the learning centers. The following procedures are the ones I rely on when determining the composition of student groups. These guidelines can be used in classrooms with learning centers or for cooperative learning in classrooms without centers. As the teacher, I assume responsibility for creating student groups. Towards the end of the school year, however, when their social skills are better developed, students may select their own group members. When working with seven groups, I determine the group size by dividing my total number of students by seven. Group sizes are typically three four or five and include:

1. **Mixed ability grouping.** I intentionally mix students together who have both low as well as high linguistic ability. I also try to mix for other skills as well. For example, I try to include at least one student with strong artistic or musical skills in each group.

2. **Mixed gender groups.** I attempt to have at least one boy and one girl in each group. Over the years, I have noted that the small groups seem to stay on task more efficiently, produce more, and have fewer social problems with mixed gender than with single sex groups.

3. **Roles emerge in groups.** Although cooperative learning experts often suggest assigning specific roles to group members, I have sometimes found this approach counterproductive. For example, Richard, whom I refer to in the introduction, might not have had an opportunity to express his musical talents if he had been assigned to serve as scribe in his cooperative groups. The one time when I do encourage assigned roles is at the Mother Teresa Center where students are intentionally practicing social skill development.

4. **One month timeframes.** While teachers select varying lengths of time for groups to stay together, I have found that starting new groups at the beginning of each month has proven most successful. It is long enough for a group to get to know each other and to learn to work well together, but short enough so that no one feels stuck in a particular group for a long period of time. By working together for only four weeks at a time, students have an opportunity to get to know everyone in the class and to practice their collaborative skills with various individuals.

5. **Groups stay together during centers.** As students move through the learning centers, they usually stay with their assigned groups. This minimizes behavior problems. I allow more flexibility with this rule as the year goes along: some students will move ahead of their groups briefly or stay behind to complete something as the situation requires.

Starting a Multiple Intelligences Program

Teachers frequently ask, "How do I get started? I like the idea of Multiple Intelligences, but I'm not sure where to begin." First of all, it is important to identify what one is already doing that incorporates some of the intelligences into student learning opportunities. It is also important to acknowledge areas that one simply overlooks or avoids! Next, teachers should realize that working with the Multiple Intelligences affects more than instructional methods. It also influences how we perceive students, how we develop curriculum, and how we assess student work. Interestingly, it also influences how we perceive ourselves as teachers. Some suggestions for getting started follow:

1. Create the environment.

One of the first steps in developing a MI classroom is to enhance the physical environment so that it can accommodate seven ways of learning. Some teachers replace student desks with tables for more space. Some simply rearrange the existing furniture so that there are spaces for small group, whole group, and individual learning. Some high school teachers team-plan curriculum and actually use each others' classrooms as needed, to take advantage of a drama stage or science lab.

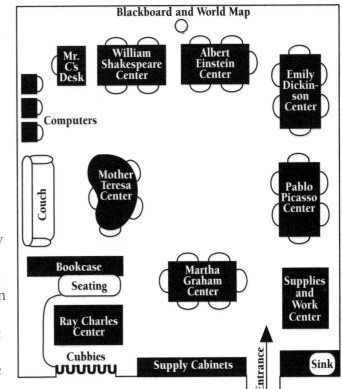

To begin my program I asked the school custodian to remove the individual desks from my classroom and to replace them with seven tables. The tables he found didn't match and were not necessarily in the best condition, however, simply having students seated at tables immediately changed my role as a frontal teacher, and gave me much more phycial space than when the room was filled with 30 individual desks. The drawing at right shows how my classroom space is organized.

In addition to changing the physical environment, a variety of MI resources must also be gathered. Hands-on materials are needed to engage each of the seven intelligences in learning. A suggested list of resources follows in the next section. Teachers must also decide how to store additional classroom resources.

2. Identify curriculum units.

In some schools, curriculum is determined by district curricular scope and sequence, by textbooks, or by teachers and students themselves. Some teachers teach thematically while others teach discrete disciplinary areas. However one approaches classroom curriculum, it is important to identify at least one major unit of focus. In my classroom, I like to create a thematic curriculum. I begin by identifying an overall theme for a unit. Next, I determine the major concepts and skills I plan to teach, and then I create individual lessons and assessment approaches. For example, a quarter-long theme I have taught was "Motion in Space and on Earth." This thematic unit addressed the structure of matter and the mechanics of objects, forces, and motion. One lesson included "What Are Asteroids and How Do They Move?" By identifying my curriculum, concepts, and lessons, I can begin planning how to incorporate the seven intelligences into student learning.

3. Identify desired outcomes.

In addition to knowing what I want to teach and what input the students will receive, I also have to identify what output I expect from my students. I need to identify what students should know and do after they have studied the unit. One of the challenges inherent in teaching through the Multiple Intelligences is finding seven ways to teach content. During my first year of MI teaching, I dedicated most of my efforts to creating activities to engage each intelligence in learning. Some of these activities were exactly that—merely activities. They did not offer valuable learning experiences for students. I quickly realized that I needed to determine what was most valuable for students to know and do. By beginning with a worthwhile outcome, I could better determine how to teach in meaningful ways. Some of the outcomes I have worked with have included writing a research report, making a collage, conducting an interview, composing a three part rhythm, or drawing a graph with X and Y coordinates.

4. Plan MI instructional strategies.

MI teaching techniques present the desired content as well as provide students with practice in essential learning skills. For example, students might learn the skill of organizing information visually while they are classifying plants and animals in their respective ecosystems. Since it takes a while to begin thinking of seven ways to teach, teachers will find lists of suggested MI strategies in Part III. These lists can serve as a resource for multimodal planning. From my own personal experience, however, I learned that planning lessons in seven modes becomes second nature after the first few months. You will experience this too!

5. Use varied assessment tools.

Just as any content can be taught in seven ways, it can also be assessed in several ways. I use a wide variety of assessment tools in my classroom. These include portfolios, art work, curriculum songs, and videotapes of student projects. Students should be involved in decision-making about assessment. Before they are to be assessed, students should, in conjunction with the teacher, identify the criteria to be used to assess their work as well as the rating scale that will be applied. When students know ahead of time what the assessment consists of they can make sure their work responds to all criteria.

6. Plan to extend each individual student's intelligence strengths.

Observe students while they are engaged in various activities. Note which activities students find enjoyable, struggle with, or even try to avoid altogether. Find ways to bridge student strengths to their areas of weakness. For example, one student of mine found mechanical tasks pleasurable, while writing seemed impossible. I asked Jason to create a dictionary of engine parts. He also went on to write a narrative explanation of how to replace oil in a car.

Plan ways to enhance student strengths. This can be easily accomplished through offering independent projects, encouraging students to participate in enrichment activities such as school clubs, or inviting experts into the classroom to work with small groups of students in apprenticeships.

7. Share your ideas.

When you are planning to work with MI in your classroom, share your intentions, efforts, and questions with colleagues, administrators, parents, and, most importantly, students for feedback and refinement.

Resources for a Multiple Intelligences Learning Environment

There are basic resources that are useful for teaching and learning in a Multiple Intelligences classroom. Many of these items already exist in most schools; they simply need to be made readily available for student use. Teachers can share and rotate resources, and students can be asked to bring items from home.

What follows is a beginning list of suggested materials to engage all seven intelligences. It is not necessary to have all items in the classroom at any one time. What is important, however, is to have a variety of resources available and to provide numerous opportunitiues for students to work with them.

I have listed the MI resources in a chart format. One column identifies resources appropriate for each intelligence. The next column may be marked with a check by those items that a teacher currently has, and the third column can star those items a teacher might like to acquire. I gathered most of my MI resources over a couple of years time with small yearly grants the district made available.

Verbal - Linguistic Resources

Resources:	Check if you already possess:	Star if you would like to acquire:
Reading materials :		
trade books		
newspapers		
reference books		
encyclopedias		
dictionaries		
thesauruses		
a variety of magazines		
student-made books		
student-selected reading materials		
bulletin and message boards		
word mobiles		
sentence strips		
pocket charts		
bilingual materials		
Writing materials:		
paper, pens, pencils		
letter stencils		
notebooks		
word processors		
desktop publishing software		
printers		
bookmaking materials		
typewriters		

16

Logical - Mathematical Resources

Resources:	Check if you already possess:	Star if you would like to acquire:
Math manipulatives:		
objects to serve as counters		
pattern blocks		
unifix cubes		
tangrams		
puzzles		
games of strategy		
blocks		
cuisinaire rods		
dice		
collections for sorting		
construction sets		
Measuring tools:		
rulers		
protractors		
tape measures		
balance scales		
measuring cups		

Kinesthetic Resources

Resources:	Check if you already possess:	Star if you would like to acquire:
Props for Skits and Movement:		
streamers		
hats, scarves, capes		
costumes		
miscellaneous props; suitcase, umbrella, etc.		
Hands-on Materials		
construction sets		
stacking blocks		
connecting blocks		
puppets		
tools		
building materials		
fabric & sewing materials		
puzzles		
board games		
craft supplies		

Visual - Spatial Resources

Resources:	Check if you already possess:	Star if you would like to acquire:
Art Materials:		
paints		
clay		
markers, crayons		
collage materials		
pastels, colored pencils		
stencils		
rubber stamps		
drafting supplies		
Visuals:		
charts		
posters		
diagrams		
graphs		
puzzles		
art prints		
flash cards		
computers		
visual software		
laser disks		
videotapes		
video equipment		

Musical Resources

Resources:	Check if you already possess:	Star if you would like to acquire:
Listening Equipment:		
records, tapes, CDs		
headphones		
recording equipment		
cassette players		
musical software		
Instruments:		
keyboards		
rhythm sticks		
tambourines		
drums		
homemade instruments		
"soft" percussion: shakers, beanbags, styrofoam, etc.		
stringed instruments		

Interpersonal Resources

Resources:	Check if you already possess:	Star if you would like to acquire:
tables instead of desks or other seating arrangements to facilitate small group work		
group games and puzzles		
problems to solve cooperatively such as learning materials that are divided up so that one group has to teach another what it knows		
board games		
software programs for cooperative work		
autobiographies and biographies		
conflict resolution personnel		
tutoring opportunities		
group projects		

Intrapersonal Resources

Resources:	Check if you already possess:	Star if you would like to acquire:
a quiet place for students to work independently		
journals		
stories, books, news articles that address character development and personal identity		
independent projects		
personal collections or artifacts		
a bulletin board or other means to acknowledge individuals for their strengths or contributions		

PART II:
PREPARING THE STUDENTS & PARENTS

Since the Theory of Multiple Intelligences is not necessarily familiar to either your students or their parents, you will need to educate both groups about the many ways there are to be intelligent.

Part II begins with a story that serves as a parable of the Multiple Intelligences. This is a story I tell to introduce Gardner's work to teachers in my workshops, but it is also a story I tell students to help them understand that there are many ways to solve problems. After the story, you will find a simple description, written for students from fourth through twelfth grade, of Gardner's theory.

Next, I include a sample letter to be sent home to parents at the beginning of the school year to explain an MI classroom program. You'll also find a student inventory that asks them to reflect on how they best like to learn, and lastly, you will find the book's first lesson plan — one on the Multiple Intelligences. It teaches students about the Multiple Intelligences by engaging all seven of their intelligences in learning.

Part II Contents:

The Prince — A Story about Multiple Intelligences

Teaching Parents and Students about the Multiple Intelligences

The Theory of Multiple Intelligences: An Explanation for Students

A Letter to Parents

Student Self-Reflection Inventory

A Seven Part Lesson on Multiple Intelligences

A Multiple Intelligences Assessment Rubric

The Prince—A Story about Multiple Intelligences

This story can be told, read, or photocopied by the teacher to introduce students to the Theory of Multiple Intelligences. It is the story of a prince who sets out on a journey and encounters diverse challenges. To resolve these challenges the prince must rely upon all seven intelligences.

For the teacher or storyteller, there are some simple materials to gather beforehand. These include:

> one small bag containing pennies (for gold coins)
>
> a small, flattened piece of clay
>
> a rock
>
> a small balance scale
>
> three balls or scarves for juggling, *(If you cannot juggle, a simple sleight of hand magic trick can be substituted to illustrate the kinesthetic problem.)*
>
> a pocket compass
>
> a small mirror,
>
> a recorder or other small flute
>
> a bag of candy containing enough pieces for each student in the class
>
> a bag to contain all of the above items

For teachers who plan to photocopy the story, you may want to delete the instructions given in italics before giving the story to your students.

THE PRINCE

There was once a young prince who lived long ago in a far-off land. As a child, the prince was taught not only riding, hunting, and swordsmanship but also letters, numbers, and music.

One day a sage (a wise old man) came into the kingdom and asked for an audience with the queen and king. The sage told the king and queen of a precious gem which had been wrongfully taken from their kingdom many years in the past. He explained that they must send their son, the prince, to reclaim it. The task would not be an easy one, for the gem was now in a distant land and it was guarded by a terrible beast with the body of a lion, the claws of a vulture, and the head of a fire-breathing serpent.

The queen and king were reluctant to send their only son on such a journey, but the sage insisted, and at last they relented. The prince prepared to leave and as he did so, his parents each gave him a gift. His father gave him a small purse filled with gold coins and told his son to use them wisely. *(Hold up small pouch with pennies.)* The prince's mother gave him a larger bag and explained that there were seven gifts inside. Each was to be used only in a time of great need. *Hold up bag containing all items except the bag of coins and the rock.)*

The prince set out and traveled for many days and nights. One evening, as he was crossing over a mountain pass, he was captured by a band of thieves. The thieves took the prince to their leader in a cave and told the youth that he must explain who he was and why he was traveling through their territory. The prince was also told that if he could explain his mission well enough to their chief, he would be allowed to continue his journey. But if he had failed, he had seen the sun rise for the last time.

Once before the chief, the prince began his story. The thieves began to laugh and it was then the prince realized their chief was deaf and heard not a word he spoke. Wondering how best to proceed, the prince reached for the first time into the bag which his mother had given him *(reach into bag)* and pulled out a small clay tablet. Quickly he wrote, "Prince, on a journey to reclaim stolen jewel." The chief, impressed by the youth's ingenuity, sent him onward to continue his journey.

The prince traveled on. Some days later, he came to a great sea which he realized he must cross. There was only one ship in port and it was skippered by an unsavory and ruthless captain who wanted no passengers aboard. The prince persisted in his requests for passage. At last the captain reached down and picked up a stone from the beach. *(Have the stone ready to pick up now.)* He told the prince that if he could precisely match the weight of that stone in gold, he would give him passage across the sea. If he failed, he would have to wait for the next ship to come — which might be several months away.

For the second time, the prince reached into the bag of seven gifts. This time he pulled out a small balance scale. He placed the stone in one side and began to count gold coins from the purse his father had given him into the other. *(Balance the scale with the stone and pennies.)* The scale balanced and the captain, like the thieves before him, was impressed with the prince's wit, and so the prince was given passage.

After a long journey across the sea, the prince came to another kingdom, where he was graciously welcomed, for the people in this land had few visitors from afar. They asked if before the prince passed through, he would first meet their king who was saddened from a turn of fortune. The townspeople hoped the prince might please their king with stories of his journey. Upon meeting the king, the prince saw that he was truly a forlorn man. Realizing the challenge before him, the prince reached for the third time into his bag and pulled out three balls. *(Pull out balls or scarves and begin to juggle.)* He began to juggle them, and the king who had never before seen such skill, was delighted, and he too gave the youth his blessing and sent him on his way.

The prince traveled on for many days, and as he did he began to hear stories of a great fortress with rich treasure inside. Tales were told of one great gem in particular which the prince knew must be the jewel which rightfully belonged to his people. As he continued, he also began to hear tales of a frightful beast inside the fortress and of many explorers who had entered, but were never seen again.

At last, the day came when the prince stood before the great fortress. The walls seemed endless, and stretched in either direction as far as the eye could see. He looked and looked but could find no entrance. While searching for a way to enter the fortress, the prince noticed an old woman struggling with a large bundle of kindling on the road. The prince rushed to help her. He carried the wood home for her and built a crackling fire.

In exchange for his generosity, the old woman not only told the boy where to find the entrance to the fortress but she also explained that once inside, he would find a great labyrinth. She warned him that many before him had entered this maze, but none had returned. If the youth were to survive, he must follow the first passage he entered to the north until he came to an opening to the east. He must then wind through this passage until he came to an opening to the south. He must follow this passage until he came to one opening to the west and so on, following this pattern until at last he would arrive at the very center.

Thanking the old woman, the prince returned to the fortress and found the entrance, but once inside lost all sense of direction. And so for the fourth time he reached into the bag his mother gave him and pulled out a small compass. Using the compass, the prince followed the directions of the old woman, north-east-south-west and so on until at last he came to the center of the labyrinth.

There in the center of the maze lay a great mound of treasure. On top was one brilliant stone which the prince recognized as the goal of his journey. But guarding the treasure was a creature more hideous than anything he had imagined. Its huge red eyes glowed, it belched fire, and around the beast were scattered the remains of others who had preceded the prince.

The creature realized someone was in the maze. It roared and began to rise. Realizing that his small sword would be of little use against this frightening beast, the prince reached into his bag and this time he pulled forth a small, wooden flute. Quickly, he began to play an old lullaby which his nursemaid had sung to him as a child. *(Play simple, soft melody on flute.)* The beast paused, and listened to the melody. As the prince continued to play, the beast, lulled by the music, slowed, stopped, and at last lay down and fell asleep. Continuing to play, the prince crept past the horrible creature, picked up the stone, which was the birthright of his land, and retraced his steps back through and out of the labyrinth.

On his homeward journey, the prince's reputation preceded him. He was called this way and that to help a traveler in distress or to aid a troubled village. One evening as he traveled down a desolate road he realized that he had wandered so far from his original path that he was entirely lost. It was then that he came upon a group of vagabonds, travelers like himself, but clearly impoverished and starving. The prince knew that they could help him, but before he could ask for help he must first do something for them. And so, reaching for the sixth time into his bag, he pulled out a smaller bag and handed it to one of the travelers who found something wonderful inside. *(Hand bag of candy to someone in the audience.)* He in turn passed the bag along to his companions and each found something of pleasure.

The travelers and the prince quickly became friends. They not only directed the prince towards his homeland but also agreed to accompany him. And so they traveled on together until the day came when the prince saw the hills of his own kingdom. But alas, one final obstacle loomed before him, for a great fissure had opened in the earth and hot lava poured forth, spreading as far as could be seen. There was nothing the prince feared more than the heat and steam of the lava and so in despair, he sat down and wondered how he could have traveled so far only to fail.

As he sat, one of his companions came up and told the prince that there was a way to cross the lava but no one could tell him what it was. He must discover it for himself. And so for the seventh and final time, he reached into the bag which his mother had given him and this time pulled out a small mirror. Looking into the mirror and seeing his reflection, the prince realized that only through his own courage and determination could he overcome this final challenge.

With new resolve, the prince stood up, picked up his bag, bade farewell to his friends and not looking down at the hot lava, but instead gazing into the distance at his homeland, he walked unharmed to the other side.

And so, the prince returned home and was welcomed as a great hero. In time, he too became king and ruled wisely and fairly. And in the years and generations that followed, he was remembered, not only for his kindness, but also for his ability to solve many problems in many ways.

After sharing this story, the teacher may want to explain Gardner's Theory of Multiple Intelligences and have the class relate the prince's challenges to each intelligence.

Teaching Parents and Students about the Multiple Intelligences

Sometimes it is useful to have a brief description of the Theory of Multiple Intelligences for students to read and to send home to parents. You may want to provide the following explanation to students as part of a lesson on Multiple Intelligences or send it home to parents to help them understand why you are teaching the way you are and what their children are talking about when they use terms such as "kinesthetic," "intrapersonal," and "Multiple Intelligence." At the end of the description I have listed some questions for students and parents to discuss.

The Theory of Multiple Intelligences: An Explanation for Students and Parents

As a teacher, I believe that there are many strengths that students possess. Not all individuals are smart in the same ways. We each have our own talents that we use and express differently from one another. Many of my ideas about how both children and adults learn are based upon The Theory of Multiple Intelligences developed by a Harvard psychologist named Howard Gardner. Gardner believes that there are at least seven ways that people can be smart. I thought you might be interested in learning more about these ideas that influence how I teach. Below, you will find an explanation for The Theory of Multiple Intelligences. First, I will begin by defining several terms:

1. A theory explains how and why certain things happen as they do. One example of a theory is, "The fact that we see lightning before we hear thunder shows that light travels faster than sound."

2. Multiple means many.

3. Intelligence is the ability to learn, to solve problems, and to become smarter.

4. A psychologist is a scientist who studies how people think and act. Howard Gardner is a psychologist at Harvard University who created a new theory of intelligence.

5. The Theory of Multiple Intelligences says that there are many ways that people can learn, solve problems, and be smart. The Theory of Multiple Intelligences was created by psychologist Howard Gardner.

In his Theory of Multiple Intelligences, Howard Gardner says that there are seven kinds of human intelligence, that people can be smart in one or more ways. Howard Gardner describes the intelligences as follows:

1. Linguistic Intelligence is the ability to think in words and use language to express ideas. Authors, poets, speakers, and newscasters are examples of people with linguistic intelligence.

2. Logical-Mathematical Intelligence is the ability to calculate, measure, use logic, and solve math and science problems. Scientists, mathematicians, accountants, and detectives are usually skilled in this intelligence.

3. Bodily-Kinesthetic Intelligence is the ability to use bodies and hands with great skill. Dancers, athletes, surgeons, jugglers, and craftspeople use this intelligence in their work.

4. Visual-Spatial Intelligence is the ability to think in pictures and to see and create images or designs with shape, color, and size. Painters, architects, sculptors, sailors, and pilots exhibit this intelligence.

5. Musical Intelligence is the ability to hear and use pitch, rhythm, and tone. Singers, musicians, composers, and skilled listeners demonstrate this intelligence.

6. Interpersonal Intelligence is the ability to understand and interact with other people in a variety of ways. Teachers, coaches, ministers, actors, social workers, and politicians all use this intelligence.

7. Intrapersonal Intelligence is the ability to understand your feelings and who you are in the world. Philosophers, psychologists, and playwrights use this intelligence.

Everyone possesses all seven intelligences. However, some of us use more of one, others more of another. The intelligences emerge at different ages so if a person is not particularly talented in one area now, he or she may actually become more intelligent in that area as he or she grows older. Also, any of these intelligences can be developed through practice and effort.

The important thing to remember is that everyone has different abilities and everyone learns and thinks in unique ways. In my classroom, I like to make sure that students have opportunities to learn in all seven ways so that each person can use his or her intelligence strengths some of the time while growing in areas that are more challenging at other times.

Some questions that are interesting for students and parents to discuss:

What are some of your favorite activities?

What intelligences do you use in your favorite activities?

What intelligences do you think are your strongest?

How did you develop these intelligences?

What role did school play in developing your intelligences?

What role did your life experiences play in developing your intelligences?

How do you use your intelligences in daily life?

Which intelligences would you like to develop more fully? Why? How would you use these intelligences?

How can schools do a better job of helping students use all their intelligences in learning?

A Letter to Parents

I have found it helpful to send a letter home to parents explaining what I am doing in my classroom and why. This letter describes my classroom and would be accompanied with the "Explanation of Multiple Intelligences for Parents and Students" above. I invariably receive return letters from parents expressing their appreciation and interest. I have never received a negative response (I'll keep my fingers crossed!).

Dear Parents,

With a new school year beginning, I want to explain my classroom to you. Each year I realize that students have their own individualized interests and abilities, so I approach every year as an adventure with new challenges. Some of those challenges are to help each student discover how he or she learns best, how to optimize their individual talents, and how to help them use their strengths to overcome their weaknesses. I organize my classroom to address these challenges.

The classroom is unique since the students work at seven learning centers each morning. They move from center to center in small groups, and at each center they learn the day's lesson in a different way. The seven ways they learn are based on a theory developed by Harvard psychologist Howard Gardner. In his book *Frames of Mind: The Theory of Multiple Intelligences*, Gardner says that everyone's mind is unique and that we all think in different ways.

I have enclosed a fact sheet on Howard Gardner's Theory of Multiple Intelligences. The students will be reading this at one of the learning centers during the first week of school. As you will see, the students in my classroom learn not only through reading, writing, and math but also through music, art, building, moving, interacting with each other, thinking, and reflecting.

In addition to their work at the centers, the students have independent projects they must work on each month. These research projects are of the students choice, and require three to four weeks to prepare. When students have completed their research, they must teach the rest of the class about what they learned using charts and diagrams, skits, music, stories, graphs, timelines, models, songs, videotapes, problems for the class to solve, and puzzles. The learning centers in my classroom teach students academic content as well as the skills of learning in seven ways. The independent projects deepen both content and skill knowledge while letting students pursue the topics that interest them the most. Project work is exciting and highly motivating for the students. I encourage you to become involved in working with your child on the research and preparation of their projects.

Finally, I am always looking for adults who are intelligent in a variety of ways to work with students in the classroom. Do you play an instrument, are you a craftsperson, do you know a lot about a particular topic, or do you just love your work? Please let me know because I would like to invite you to come in and share your talents or interests with the class. In fact, I invite you to come in just to visit, ask questions, and learn more about what we are doing.

I look forward to working with both you and your student this year!

Sincerely Yours,

Student Self-Reflection Inventory

After students have been introduced to The Theory of Multiple Intelligences, you may be interested in having them respond to this inventory. The inventory asks students to reflect on their current strengths. It will provide you with useful information about how they like to learn, and how they perceive their strengths.

If you administer this inventory before you begin teaching through the seven intelligences it will provide you with baseline data to compare how students change throughout the course of the year.

In my own classroom, after administering the inventory at the beginning of the school year, I find that students prefer to learn in two to four ways. As they have opportunities to learn in all seven intelligences over the course of the year, their learning preferences increase.

You may want to administer this inventory at the beginning of the year and once or twice throughout the year to determine how students' learning preferences as well as their perceptions of their talents have changed.

YOUR CURRENT LEARNING PREFERENCES

Name: _____

1. What is your favorite subject at school? _____

2. What do you like to spend your time doing at home?
   _____

3. How do you like to learn about things (reading, drawing, acting things out, etc.) _____

4. Check all of the things you think you are good at:
   ____ Reading
   ____ Discussing
   ____ Journal writing, poetry, other kinds of writing
   ____ Music (singing, rhythm, listening, playing instruments)
   ____ Art (drawing, painting, sculpting, collage, etc.)
   ____ Math (calculating, solving story problems, measuring, etc.)
   ____ Movement activities (acting, dancing, juggling, etc.)
   ____ Building activities (constructing things from any materials)
   ____ Working with others
   ____ Working alone and thinking about things

5. List other things you think you do well that are not listed above:
   _____

6. What do you think is your strongest intelligence? Check one:
   Linguistic_____   Mathematical _____
   Kinesthetic _____   Visual _____
   Musical _____   Interpersonal_____
   Inrapersonal _____

7. What would you like to be better at? _____

8. What do you think you are getting better at?_____

9. What subjects would you like to learn more about? _____

10. What other thoughts or suggestions do you have to make school _ or this class more interesting? _____
    _____

A Seven Part Lesson on Multiple Intelligences

This is the book's first lesson plan. It is offered here because it serves as an introduction for students about the seven intelligences. The suggested activities can be presented in any order and can be taught through direct instruction or at seven centers. I have written the directions for each of the centers to the students. If you are interested, you may simply photocopy the seven activities and give them to your students.

Subject Area:	Psychology/Health, Thinking skills
Main Concept:	Human intelligence is multi-faceted
Principle To Be Taught:	Individuals have unique cognitive profiles
Unit:	Our bodies, our brains, our abilities
Grade levels:	3-12

Materials Needed:

Photocopy and make available to students the

1. The Theory of Multiple Intelligences for Students and Parents (above) for the linguistic activity
2. Logical-mathematical story problem for all students
3. One copy of each fact sheet of the seven famous people for the interpersonal activity
4. One copy of the intrapersonal questions for each student
5. One blank copy of the pie chart for the visual-spatial activity for each student
6. Enough simple musical instruments for students to work with in small groups

Linguistic Activity:

Read the description, The Theory of Multiple Intelligences for Students . After reading the information, discuss the following:
• What does it mean to be smart?
• Which intelligences do you think are your strongest?
• Who do you know who is smart in one or more intelligences?

Logical - Mathematical Activity:

Solve the following problem:

Gabriel, Daniel, Gracie, Maria, Li, Kumar, and Jamal are at Jamal's house trying to solve a problem their teacher has given them. Each of the students is particularly talented in one form of intelligence.

Gabriel is the most physically active and likes to move around while solving the problem. Neither Maria nor Li like to be alone. Gracie asks Jamal to turn the stereo off. Daniel doesn't like solving problems unless he can use some kind of formula. Kumar brought all her art supplies. Li brought a pile of books. Jamal is busy organizing the whole group.

Can you tell which student relies upon which intelligence? List their individual strengths below:

Gabriel _____   Gracie _____
Daniel _____   Li _____
Jamal _____   Kumar_____
Maria _____

Kinesthetic Activity:

In a small group, brainstorm a list of jobs that require physical skills such as carpenters or surgeons. Identify two of these jobs and create brief silent pantomimes for each that show the activities people perform in such jobs. Prepare to show other students your two pantomimes and have them guess what job your group is portraying.

Visual-Spatial Activity:

Make a pie chart of your seven intelligences. Divide the circle into seven sections with each section representing by its size how talented you are in that intelligence.

For example, you may want to make a large section for linguistic intelligence if you like to read, write, and talk, and a small section for musical intelligence if you do not sing, play instruments, or listen to music very much.

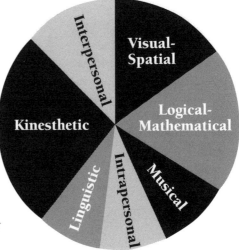

Musical Activity:

Using the instruments provided, create a rhythm to accompany the following lyrics:

Multiple Intelligences are really cool.
It means that nobody is a fool.
Everyone can sing his or her own praise,
Because we are smart in so many ways.

Interpersonal Activity

Break into small groups. In your small group, ask one person to read a fact sheet out loud about a famous person who demonstrated a particular intelligence. After the fact sheet has been read, discuss:
1. what intelligence this person demonstrated,
2. how this person expressed his or her intelligence,
3. why he or she was famous, and
4. other people you know who possess similar strengths

William Shakespeare

William Shakespeare was an English writer who lived 400 years ago. He wrote poems and plays and is considered the greatest dramatist (a person who writes plays) and the greatest English language poet who ever lived. He is still the most popular author in the world. His plays have been performed thousands of times in countries around the world.

Some of his most famous plays are *Richard III, Romeo and Juliet, Macbeth, Hamlet,* and *A Midsummer Night's Dream.* He wrote three kinds of plays: comedies, tragedies, and histories. *A Midsummer Night's Dream* is a comedy, *Macbeth* is a tragedy, and *Richard III* is a historical play.

The reason that Shakespeare is so famous is because he understood people and their life experiences. The characters in his plays appeal to audiences because they address situations similar to ones many of us encounter in our daily lives such as jealousy, a struggle for power, or love at first sight.

Albert Einstein

Albert Einstein was one of the greatest scientists who ever lived. He studied time, space, mass, motion, and gravity. He is famous for his equation $E=mc^2$ (Energy = mass times the speed of light squared) which suggests that matter and energy are equal. Understanding this equation made it possible for scientists to develop atomic energy and the atomic bomb.

Einstein developed his theories not only through mathematical calculations but also through deep, reflective thinking. He was very interested in philosophy, music, and politics. He believed strongly in world peace even though his ideas led to the development of the atomic bomb.

Before Einstein, scientists believed that light was a kind of wave. Einstein suggested that light could be thought of as a tiny stream of particles called *quanta*. This discovery led to the invention of movies and television.

One of Einstein's most famous discoveries is the theory of relativity which is about time and space. He determined that if a space traveler were to leave Earth and travel far out into space, when he returned he would be younger than if he had remained on Earth.

Martha Graham

Martha Graham was an American dancer and choreographer (someone who creates dances). She invented "modern dance" and used her entire body in dance movements to express her inner feelings and thoughts. Many of her dances did not appear graceful because some of the feelings she expressed, such as anger, fear, and hatred, called for rough and jagged motions. During the 1930's, 1940's, and 1950's, Martha Graham's dances shocked audiences with their unique style. Yet because of the dances she created, people began to look at this art form in new ways.

Graham began dancing as a girl in the early 1900's and continued to dance for over eighty years. Many of her dances described the life experiences of women, myths, and people from rural America, and diverse cultures. She said that dance made our inner feelings visible.

Pablo Picasso

Picasso was the most famous painter of this century. He created new styles of art, and often, when one style became accepted, Picasso would create an entirely new form. He responded to the changing conditions in the world during the 20th century and to his own changing feelings. His art reflected these transformations.

Picasso's paintings seemed to be filled with strange and distorted images, ones that might be glimpsed in nightmares. In using these images, he seemed to be trying to connect the viewer with his or her own inner thoughts and feelings. Much of Picasso's art was influenced by the art of his home country of Spain. One of his most famous paintings, Guernica, is about the bombing of a town in Spain during the Spanish Civil War.

One of his earliest stages as a painter is called the "Blue Period," since many of his paintings at that time included a great deal of blue. Next, Picasso switched to warm colors and expressed a variety of moods in his paintings. He went through a stage of painting circus scenes, and then huge, massive figures. Next his paintings became so jagged and distorted that it was difficult to identify who or what was in the paintings. In a later stage, Picasso began to include newspaper clippings, words, and pieces of debris in his work. In addition to his paintings, Picasso is also famous for his sculpture, ceramics, and drawings.

Ray Charles

Ray Charles is a black American singer and songwriter. He rose to popularity in the 1950's as a jazz singer and continues to be one of the best known American pop singers. His soft drink commercials have made him popular recently with people of all ages.

Charles became blind since the age of six. He plays the piano and sings with emotion and enthusiasm. His songs range from rock to blues. *I Got A Woman* was the hit song that propelled him to the forefront of American music. *What I Say* and *Georgia On My Mind* are two other well known hits.

Early in his career he sang with several bands, but recently he has preferred to do solo performances. Although in his sixties, Ray Charles continues to perform concerts around the world.

Mother Teresa

Mother Teresa is a Roman Catholic nun who lives in India and works with the poor, starving, and sick people of Calcutta. She began a religious order in India over forty years ago to provide hospitals, schools, shelters, orphanages, and youth centers for people who were hungry, sick, or dying. Her work has branched out to over fifty cities in India and over thirty countries around the world.

Mother Teresa was born in Yugoslavia and became a nun at the age of eighteen. In 1948, she left her convent and went to Calcutta, one of the poorest cities in the world. Here she was inspired to attend to those in greatest need. Her work has earned her numerous awards and prizes. In 1979, she received the Nobel peace prize for her work helping the poor. This prize is generally given to presidents and world leaders and is considered the highest humanitarian award in the world.

Emily Dickinson

Emily Dickinson was a great American poet who lived in the 1800's. She is still considered one of the finest poets to write in the English language.

She lived most of her life secluded in her family home in Massachusetts. She never married and had very few friends. She spent her time alone, pondering her deepest feelings, and writing about them. Those who have studied her work suggest that because she spent so much time examining her feelings, she was able to write about them in unique ways.

Her poems were generally short and had no titles. Most of them were sad and dealt with loneliness, anxiety, and death. She also wrote about the soul, God, and immortality. Dickinson wrote over 1,700 poems but only seven of them were published during her lifetime, and those seven without her permission. She wrote secretly; her sister discovered her work after the poet died.

Intrapersonal Activity:

Now that you have been introduced to the idea of Multiple Intelligences, analyze your individual strengths and abilities. Think silently for a few minutes and then with your group members discuss one or more of the following questions:

- What do you perceive as your strongest area of intelligence?

- How did you develop this strength?

- How do you use this ability?

- How could you improve your expertise in this area?

- In what new way could you use your ability?

- What new intelligence would you like to develop?

Assessment

To show your understanding of the Theory of Multiple Intelligences, prepare a demonstration about MI for your class. You may work independently or with one or two other students. Your demonstration should include one or more of the following elements:

1. A short skit or interview demonstrating that different people are smart in at least seven different ways.

2. A poster with labels and pictures of each of the seven intelligences. The pictures can be drawn or cut from magazines.

3. A brief narrative description of the theory with examples of famous people others will recognize.

4. Some type of questionnaire that the class can use to identify their own areas of intelligence.

5. A song about MI which mentions all seven intelligences and how people can be smart in these ways.

The rubric on the next page can be used to evaluate the effectiveness of your demonstration.

Multiple Intelligences Lesson Rubric

Scoring Scale:	Excellent	Adequate	Not Evident
CRITERIA:			
Presented all seven intelligences			
Showed understanding of the seven intelligences			
Was clear and easy to understand			
Was interesting as well as informative			

PART III: PREPARING FOR MI TEACHING

Many teachers are interested in teaching through the seven intelligences. Yet human nature appears to dictate that we teach from our areas of strength and avoid modes that are uncomfortable to us.

This section of the handbook asks teachers to reflect on their current modes of instruction, and to consider the support they might need to teach in additional modes. I then attempt to provide support for multiple-intelligences-based pedagogy by offering a variety of instructional strategies for each intelligence. Teachers may want to review each list by checking off strategies currently used and starring those that could be easily incorporated into daily teaching. For each intelligence, I also describe one instructional strategy in greater depth. At the end of this section, teachers will find two student handouts, one on spelling and one on multiplication, that integrate all seven intelligences into these two essential basic skill areas.

Part III Contents:

Teacher Self-Reflection Inventory
Linguistic Strategies and Journaling
Logical/ Mathematical Strategies and a Deductive Reasoning Game
Bodily/ Kinesthetic Strategies and Paper Plates
Visual/Spatial Strategies and Student-made Cards
Musical Strategies and Curriculum Songs
Interpersonal Strategies and Mix-and-Match Grouping
Intrapersonal Strategies and Student Choice Options
Student Handouts:
      Spelling Worksheet
      Multiplication Worksheet

Teacher Self-Reflection Inventory

The following inventory is offered as a way to reflect on how you currently teach. After taking the inventory, review it to see which intelligences you overlook in your instruction. You may want to focus on any neglected areas by incorporating instructional strategies suggested in the following pages of this handbook.

My primary intelligence strengths are:
1. _____
2. _____
3. _____

The content I teach typically engages the following intelligences (Note if there is any correlation with #1 above. If yes, why? If no, why not?)
1. _____
2. _____
3. _____
4. _____
5. _____

The intelligences I typically teach through include:
1. _____
2. _____
3. _____

Examples for each of the above:
1. _____
2. _____
3. _____

One or more intelligences I usually overlook are:
1. _____   2. _____

The reason for such oversight is:
_____
_____

I would be willing to teach through that intelligence if:
_____
_____

Resources for doing so would include:
_____
_____

Linguistic Strategies

1. For five minutes, students do "quick writes" reacting to lesson information.

2. Students tell stories of how they apply ideas from any discipline to their lives outside of school.

3. To practice accuracy in communication, pairs of students listen to each other giving directions for an assignment .

4. To learn vocabulary for any topic, students create crossword puzzles.

5. Students debate diverse perspectives of any issue.

6. Students describe in writing the most meaningful content they have studied.

7. In small groups, students give impromptu, one minute presentations to each other on topics of the teacher's choice drawn from current lessons.

8. When reading classroom material, students review each page by creating keywords or phrases for the content of that page.

9. Students create mini-talk show programs where they pose as junior experts on classroom topics.

10. Using a word that represents a major concept, such as interdependence, students write a phrase with each letter of the word to explain its meaning.

Sample Linguistic Activity: Journal Writing

Journals can be integrated into any subject area. Students can maintain journals for numerous purposes: to explain lesson content or problem-solving approaches, to express feelings about the content studied, to raise questions about what they don't understand, or to express concerns directly to the teacher. Before assigning journals, teachers may want to determine whether students are writing them in other classes. Several types of journals are described below to add variety to this worthwhile linguistic strategy:

1. Learning Logs
In learning logs, students record the key concepts, supporting details, or problem-solving processes of their curriculum unit. They can be written in daily, weekly, or spontaneously, on occasion.

2. Personal Journals

In personal journals, students determine the form and content of their own entries. They record their thoughts and feelings much like a diary. Some students may choose to write stories or poetry, or their dreams, fears, or wishes. Some teachers request that students write in personal journals on a daily basis.

3. Notebook Journals

Leonardo da Vinci recorded his ideas in notebook journals. Such journals evolve out of the interests of the students, and may take many forms such as visual sketchbooks or statistical charting. Notebook journals are used on a spontaneous basis.

4. Dialogue Journals

Dialogue journals are generally shared with the teacher or other students. The student begins a story or narrative and the teacher or a classmate responds. The response can be a personal comment or a continuation of the story. This is time-consuming for teachers but motivating for students. Students usually write in dialogue journals on pre-scheduled days of the week.

5. Simulation Journals

In simulation journals, the student assumes the role of another person: an author, historical figure, scientist, imaginary character, animal, or inanimate object. These journals are used to help students understand diverse perspectives, and are often assigned at irregular intervals.

6. Reading Journals

These journals record students' understanding, interpretation, critique, and analysis of their readings. They are contributed to during and upon completion of assigned readings.

7. Class Journals

Class journals are contributed to by everyone in the classroom. A single journal is maintained on a podium or table for students, teachers, and guests to write entries on specified or spontaneous topics. These journals definitely motivate students to read and write.

Logical-Mathematical Strategies

1. When given a problem, students plan strategies for ways to solve the problem before attempting its resolution.

2. Students are asked to discern patterns or relationships in lesson contents.

3. When offering solutions to any problem, students must provide a logical rationale to support their answers.

4. Students create or identify categories for sorting diverse data.

5. To extend classroom learning, students conduct surveys and analyze data on topics that they or the teacher have selected.

6. Working in pairs, students make up story problems involving lesson content.

7. Students engage in discussions which include higher level thinking skills, such as comparing and contrasting, providing cause and effect answers, analyzing, hypothesizing, and synthesizing information.

8. As an independent or small group project, students employ the scientific method to answer a question they have about a classroom topic.

9. Students study units focused on math and science themes such as probability, symmetry, randomness, and chaos.

10. Students use a variety of organizers to enhance logical thinking, such as outline charts, Venn Diagrams, flow charts, and mindmaps.

Sample Logical-Mathematical Activity: A Deductive Reasoning Game

Nearly everyone is familiar with the Jeopardy™ game show, which provides answers instead of questions. Players must determine the appropriate question for each answer given. The same process can be used effectively in the classroom with any subject area. As long as you can think of questions, you can play Jeopardy™.

The format is up to the teacher. Some teachers list answers on the board and let students or groups raise their hands, choose an answer, and state the question when called upon. Others will hand out cards to cooperative groups and have each group answer their own. Some teachers will provide a worksheet of answers for students to find matching questions.

Regardless of the format, students must use logical reasoning to determine the appropriate question. The questions may be relatively simple: Category—continents—*Antarctica* (What is the coldest continent?) Or they can be more complex: Category—Biology—*Mitosis* (What is the sequential differentiation and segregation of replicated chromosomes in a cell nucleus that precedes complete cell division?) Or they can involve higher level thinking skills: Category—Environmental Science—*The Energy Crisis* (What has the overuse of earth's energy sources and the increased demand for power created?)

Kinesthetic Strategies

1. Students role play any process such as photosynthesis, making a bill into a law, solving a quadratic equation, or the earth's orbit around the sun.

2. Working together, with small blocks, toothpicks, legos, or popsicle sticks, students build models of molecular chains, famous bridges, or towns in history or literature.

3. Teachers can provide quick exercise breaks with simple calisthenics, Tai Chi or yoga stretches, an active game of Simon Says, or even a jog around the playground.

4. In small groups, students can create large floor games that cover important concepts being studied.

5. Students can enact simulations, such as groups representing countries with different resources to trade, or pioneers addressing the challenges of the frontier.

6. Teachers can create "scavenger hunts" as one way for students to gather information on particular topics.

7. Regardless of the content, teachers may provide manipulatives for students to use to solve math problems, create patterns for art work, build replicas of cells or systems, or make storyboards for language and writing experiences.

8. To extend classroom learning into the community, students go on field trips.

9. Students learn physical skills like juggling, dancing, balancing, rope jumping, climbing, hula-hooping, bowling, throwing, catching, or working with tools of various kinds.

10. Students pantomime what they have learned from a day's lesson.

Sample Kinesthetic Activity: "Paper Plates"

This is a simple, active game to review any topic. To prepare, obtain paper plates. Second, identify your topic and write down 5 to 10 pertinent questions with one-word answers. Third, write the answers to your questions on the plates, with 3 to 5 plates having the same answer. Now you are ready for any number of students to play.

Scatter the plates, answer side up, around the room. Explain to students that you will read a question and they must find the paper plate that correctly answers that question. When they locate it, they must put a finger or toe on the plate as quickly as possible. When everyone has found a correct answer-plate, read another question and off they go again.

There are two simple rules for game playing:

1. Students cannot touch anyone else (which makes it challenging when several students head for the same plate).

2. Students cannot make any noise (otherwise it will not be possible hear the questions being read).

Four examples of paper plate games are shown below:

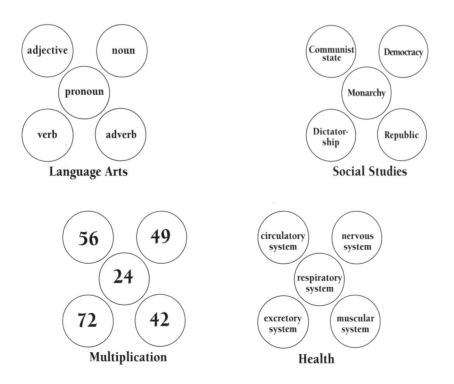

Visual-Spatial Strategies

1. Students might experiment with imagery to mentally rehearse performing well on a test, speaking in front of the class, or successfully resolving a conflict.

2. Students create a pictorial representation of what they have learned from a unit of study such as a chart, drawing, or mindmap.

3. Working independently or with a partner, students create a visual collage to display facts, concepts, and questions they have about a recent unit of study.

4. With access to computer graphics and page-layout programs, students illustrate their lessons.

5. Students diagram the structures of interconnecting systems such as body systems, economic systems, political systems, school systems, or food chains.

6. To communicate their understanding of a topic, students create flow charts, bar graphs, or pie charts.

7. Working in small groups, students create videotape or photograph projects.

8. To work with three-dimensional activities, students design costumes or sets for literature or social studies, tools or experiments for science, and manipulatives or new classroom or building designs for math.

9. Students create mobiles or design bulletin boards.

10. To demonstrate their understanding of a topic, students use color, shape, or rebus-type images in their papers.

Sample Visual-Spatial Activity: Student-made Cards

Nearly anything can be learned or reviewed with student-made cards. These can be artistic flash cards using colors, shapes, and designs to make them visually interesting and memorable.

Cards can also be used to make simple games. Rummy, "Go Fish," or "Old Maid" games can be adapted to any subject area. Simply cut up card stock, construction paper, or note cards, plan your game based upon the subject area, and have students mark and illustrate the cards. A rubber stamp can give them uniformity on one side. A laminator can make them durable.

Commercial games of authors, artists, scientists, explorers, and inventors are available in many catalogs and educational supply houses. However, the best ones are those that teachers or students make.

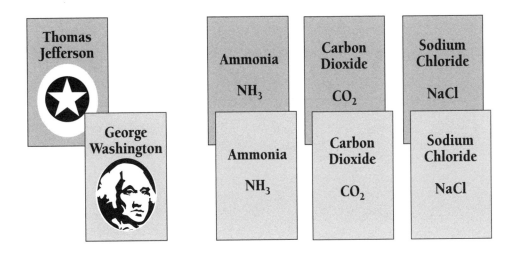

Musical Strategies

1. Teachers play background music to relax students or to focus their attention at various times during the day.

2. To review information, students compose curriculum songs, replacing the words to well-known songs with content information.

3. Students make their own rhythm instruments to use with curriculum songs or recitations of arithmetic facts, spelling words, or sets of rules or facts.

4. Students select a song and explain how its lyrics relate to a lesson's content.

5. For students with access to musical software, rhythmic accompaniment can be added to multimedia reports and presentations.

6. Students select appropriate background music for book reports or other oral presentations.

7. To demonstrate patterns in mathematics, nature, and the visual arts, students use musical selections that are patterned and repetitive.

8. To become knowledgeable in any subject area, students listen to and analyze pre-recorded songs about the content areas.

9. Students analyze music to understand concepts such as relationships of parts to wholes, fractions, repeating patterns, timing, and harmony.

10. Students use musical vocabulary as metaphors such as crescendo for the climax of a short story; two-part harmony for interpersonal relations; or cadence for physical exercise.

Sample Musical Activity: Curriculum Songs

In addition to enhancing classroom ambiance, it is important to include music in the curriculum. Tapes with songs in the content areas are available through educational materials catalogs for nearly any subject. Even more effective are teacher-made and student-made songs about topics being studied. Here is an example of a song about environmental pollution composed by a group of third graders after a lesson on the ozone layer. It is sung to the tune of *"Jingle Bells."*

Jingle bells, garbage smells,
Diapers in the dump.
Styrofoam and CFC's,
They make me scream and jump, oh

Jingle bells, garbage smells,
Pollution is a drag.
Toxic wastes from factories
Make me want to gag.

Students can be organized into small groups to write an entire song or to contribute a stanza to a class song. Students should be directed to select a song with a familiar tune. The teacher can also specify expectations such as including 10 concepts from a recent unit of study or including questions the class still wants answered about a topic. Once students have written their songs, they should have opportunities to sing and teach them to the whole class.

A list of familiar songs follows. These all have simple and recognizable rhythms which can be used to provide the melody for curriculum songs.

Michael Row the Boat Ashore	When Johnny Comes Marching Home
She'll Be Comin' Round the Mountain	The Battle Hymn of the Republic
This Old Man	The Old Gray Mare
Pop Goes the Weasel	Alouette
Clementine	My Country Tis of Thee
Oh, Susannah	Camptown Races
Wheels on the Bus	I've Been Working on the Railroad
London Bridge	Hava Nagila
Jimmy Crack Corn	Puff, The Magic Dragon
This Land is Your Land	Sarasponda
Twinkle, Twinkle Little Star	We Shall Overcome
Yankee Doodle	When the Saints Come Marching In

Interpersonal Strategies

1. Working in cooperative groups, students teach each other parts of a lesson. Each student is responsible for teaching only one part, while everyone learns the whole lesson collaboratively.
2. To develop the ability to resolve disputes and negotiate conflicts, students practice conflict resolution techniques with either simulated or actual problems.
3. Students practice critiquing one another's work to learn how to give and receive feedback.
4. To build collaborative skills and to share each other's areas of expertise, students work on group projects together, each assuming a role according to his or her strengths.
5. Students engage in school or community service activities to develop values such as empathy, respect, altruism, and sharing.
6. To understand others and appreciate differences, students study diverse cultures, including customs, beliefs, and values.
7. Use the "Think-Pair-Share" technique to engage students in reflecting upon a class topic and then discussing their thoughts with a partner.
8. To understand differing points of view, students assume various positions and debate a complex issue.
9. Students interview persons with special talents to learn about their areas of specialty as well as how to interview others effectively.
10. To learn from the expertise of others, students work as apprentices with community experts.

Sample Interpersonal Activity: Mix-&-Match Grouping

This grouping activity works well when introducing new material. Organize students into groups of four to five. Hand out a set of numbered (1-5) fact cards to each group. Each card within a set should have different information about your subject but each group's set of cards should be the same.

Students read their cards then move to new groups with matching numbers. (All the 1's get together, all the 2's get together, etc.) These groups then plan a strategy to teach their original groups what they have learned from their cards.

When the groups are ready, each student returns to her or his original group. Now everyone has a different piece of the puzzle and a method for teaching it. Individuals take turns sharing their "piece" with their group.

Intrapersonal Strategies

1. At the beginning of a course, school year or semester, students establish personal short- and long-term learning goals.

2. Students maintain portfolios to evaluate their own learning.

3. Using schedules, timelines, and planning strategies, students choose and direct some of their own learning activities to gain autonomous learning skills.

4. Students keep daily learning logs where they express their emotional reactions to lessons as well as share any insights they have into the content.

5. Students explain why certain units of study are valuable for them both inside and outside of school.

6. Students select a particular value such as kindness or determination and incorporate that value into their behavior for a week at a time.

7. To enhance self-esteem, students practice giving and receiving compliments from one another.

8. At least once per quarter, students pursue an independent project of their choice spanning 2-3 weeks.

9. Students write autobiographies to explain how class content has enhanced their understanding of themselves.

10. Students use teacher feedback and self-assessment inventories to reflect on their individual learning, thinking, and problem-solving strategies.

Sample Intrapersonal Activity: Student Options

One approach to empowering students academically while developing intrapersonal skills is to encourage them to make choices involving their educational experiences. Choices can be open-ended, based upon student interests, or they can be provided by the teacher. A few suggestions are listed below for enabling students to construct their learning experiences.

- Let students decide how best to organize the classroom's physical layout.

- Allow students choices of topics for reading and writing assignments.

- Provide students with a range of options for independent research projects.

- Seek student input for the daily schedule.

- Ask students to develop rules and discipline policies for common problems that arise.

- Let students choose seating arrangements.

- Teach students how to set goals for themselves and provide opportunities for them to complete goals they have set.

- Provide frequent opportunities for self-reflection and self-evaluation.

- Supply students with personal journals and plan a regular journal writing time.

- Ask students to determine the criteria by which their work will be assessed.

To begin Multiple Intelligence-based teaching, many teachers select intelligence strategies listed above and put them together in a worksheet so that students have multiple ways to learn academic content. Two sample worksheets are provided on the following pages: one on spelling and one on multiplication.

Multiple Intelligences Spelling

The following list provides you with a variety of ways to practice spelling words at school and at home. Select the strategies that you enjoy most. Vary the strategies each week. Try to determine which approaches helped you learn the spelling words the best.

- Create categories for your spelling words. For example, one category might be to group all words containing eight letters. Another might be to group words with more than one e. See how many categories you can create.
  (logical-mathematical intelligence strategy)

- Write your words using different colors for the letters or parts of the word that are confusing to you.
  (visual intelligence strategy)

- Make up a story using all spelling words. Tell the story to another person, stopping to spell each spelling word.
  (linguistic strategy)

- Sing-spell your words to the melody of your favorite song.
  (musical intelligence strategy)

- Create a body alphabet of letters and pantomime each letter of each spelling word
  (kinesthetic intelligence strategy)

- With a partner, use the "Think, Pair, Share" technique to practice your spelling words.
  (interpersonal intelligence strategy)

- Create your own goals for how you will study and learn your spelling words.
  (intrapersonal strategy)

Multiple Intelligences Multiplication

The following list provides you with a variety of ways to practice multiplication at school and at home. Select the strategies that you enjoy the most. Vary the strategies each week. Try to determine which approaches helped you learn multiplication the best.

- With a partner, play the Paper Plate game to practice your multiplication facts. Write answers to the times tables, one per plate, and place the plates on the floor. Have your partner call out a statement such as 6 x 3. You jump onto the plate with the answer of 18.
  (kinesthetic and interpersonal intelligences)

- Make artistic flash cards for each multiplication fact. For example, you might want to draw a design of 24 flowers on one side of the card and on the flip side have the statement 6 x 4.
  (visual intelligence)

- Make up mini - stories with multiplication facts in them. For example, one story might begin .....There once was a boy who played basketball and scored four points per basket.
  (linguistic intelligence)

- When looking at a chart of the multiplication facts, find at least two number patterns in the chart.
  (logical-mathematical strategy)

- Select background music to play during study times that will help you concentrate on your multiplication facts.
  (musical strategy)

- Interview other people to find out how they memorized the multiplication tables. Take tips from them that will help you to memorize these math facts.
  (interpersonal strategy)

- Keep a daily log to express your feelings about learning the multiplication tables and to track which facts you learn each day.
  (intrapersonal intelligence)

PART IV:
ASSESSMENT IN AN
MI CLASSROOM

In my own classroom, I have found it necessary to design alternative assessment processes that reflect the MI work of my students. I learned that it is valuable to engage in "collaborative assessment conferences" with my students so that they have input into the criteria by which their work is assessed. I have developed portfolio processes, evaluation forms, self-reflection sheets, and MI- report cards to record student progress. You will find such methods of assessment included in this section.

I would also like to point out that just as we can teach in seven ways, we can also assess in seven ways. MI- assessments can take a variety of forms. Students can demonstrate their learning through original songs, culminating essays, performances and projects, or visuals, such as charts, diagrams, or timelines. In addition, a teacher's assessment repertoire should include peer- and self-assessment processes. For numerous examples of assessment ideas, consult the assessment sections of each lesson plan included in this book.

Whenever I assess my students, I also remind myself that evaluation serves many purposes. First, it documents student progress and provides a way to communicate to students and others about that progress. Assessment is an important feedback tool, not just about student progress, but also about my effectiveness as a teacher. It encourages me to reflect on what works in my teaching and what needs to improve. Assessment also gives me insight into the strengths and challenges of each student and asks me to identify appropriate interventions. In my mind, assessment is an ongoing dialogue, not a final summative event.

Part IV Contents:

An MI Rubric
Collaborative Assessment Conferences
MI Portfolios
Personal Reflection Sheets
Peer Assessment with the "Appreciation Sandwich"
Long-term Student Project Assessment
An MI Report Card

An MI Rubric

Teachers are often busy creating both teaching and assessing materials for each curriculum unit they cover. I have found it convenient at times to have a "generic" rubric ready for quick adapting to any lesson I teach. I've developed the following rubric for just such a purpose. It can be completed by teacher, students, or both. It can also serve as a cover sheet for a portfolio item.

Student Name: _____

Assignment: _____

Date: _____

Content:	Outstanding	Good	Fair	Needs Work
Demonstrated understanding of important concepts				
Provided examples of important concepts				
Applied content to other areas or real life situations				
Responded to questions when asked				

Skills:				
Showed evidence of research skills				
Effectively communicated content to audience				
Used at least 3 intelligences in presentation				
Articulated challenges in completing assignment				

The Collaborative Assessment Conference

The collaborative assessment conference, originally designed by Rieneke Zessoules and Steve Seidel for Arts PROPEL, is a dialogue between student and teacher about important student work. It democratizes the assessment process by giving those who are being assessed an opportunity to say what the assessment should look like, and, upon completion of their work, how they think they met such criteria. The assumption of this conference is that serious student work deserves serious teacher attention and response. Collaborative assessment conferences have two aspects: the first is to determine criteria for assessing student work, and the second is to reflect in depth on the effectiveness of that work.

Establishing Assessment Criteria:

Before students tackle an important assignment or major project, the teacher and students should hold an assessment conference. This will require from ten to thirty minutes of discussion. The purpose of the conference is to establish the criteria for assessing student work. As the class discusses what assessment should consist of, the teacher should list the criteria upon the board. It is important that these criteria address both content and skill development. For example, one requirement might be that the completed assignment reveals a clear understanding of an important concept; a second requirement might be that the concept is effectively presented through a graph, chart, or diagram, or is applied to a real world situation.

By establishing the criteria in advance, students have guidelines for their work. They no longer need to guess at what the teacher wants, and they know exactly what their responsibilities entail. It is also helpful if teachers have samples of previous student work to share as models. By seeing what others have done, students are in a better position to make decisions about what they might do. Rather than encouraging copying, sample student work encourages students to build upon the ideas of others and to forge their own original problem-solving approaches. It often significantly increases the quality of student effort and product.

Assessing Student Work

Upon completion of an important assignment, the second collaborative assessment conference is scheduled. The intent of this conference is to provide the student with feedback about the quality of the work, how well the criteria were met, and how the teacher can help the student further achieve what he or she is trying to accomplish. Occasionally other participants, such as teachers, specialists, parents, or other students, may also be included in this conference. These conferences can be conducted with individual students or with the entire class observing and participating. Before the assessment conference begins, it is critical that the teacher has previously read or examined the assignment in order to be prepared to discuss it. During the conference, it is important that the student who completed the work discuss his product.

I have suggested some topics below that may be helpful to the teacher in conducting an assessment conference:

1. In the simplest terms and without judgment, describe what the student has created.

2. Suggest what is most striking to you about this project. The focus here should be upon the description and not upon "why" the student completed the work in such a manner.

3. Share questions about the work and the student that occur to you when you look at, listen to, or read this product.

4. Evaluate how the work addresses the required criteria.

During the conference, the student and other participants should be encouraged to discuss the work. This can be facilitated with questions like: "Were there any surprises to you in the comments I have made?" "Do you have any observations you would like to add?" "Are there aspects of your work that I have missed?"

To conclude a collaborative assessment conference, suggest next steps in the student's learning. Even though the student has a finished product, one of the important concepts to communicate is that learning is an ongoing and never-ending process. Some comments and questions might include:

1. I believe this work demonstrates that you have a strength in
   _____ that you can apply to other work.

2. Do you have additional interests that you would like to pursue because of this project?

3. Now that you have completed this assignment, what aspects of it could be strengthened?

4. What would encourage you to do high quality work in the future?

5. What forms could your future work take?

In closing the conference, it is often worthwhile to discuss the conference itself. How did it work for everyone involved? How could it be improved? Finally, it is important to end on a positive note. Comments such as, "I can tell you worked hard on collecting the information for this assignment," or "I can see that you learned a lot from creating your chart" are helpful in encouraging ongoing effort.

MI Portfolios

Portfolios are purposeful collections of student work that are becoming increasingly popular with both elementary and secondary teachers. I have experimented with portfolio systems that involve a Collection Folder which includes all student work and a Showcase Portfolio with only selected pieces. When selecting pieces for placement in a portfolio, it is important to have a combination of teacher-chosen work and student-chosen work.

I have also experimented with different categories of portfolios depending upon the subject area. At times, I have asked my students to maintain a single subject or topic portfolio such as a Science Portfolio or a Writing Portfolio. At other times, I have worked with comprehensive portfolios that incorporate work from all content areas. In either case, the portfolio can cover the work of one term, an entire year, or it can follow the student from year to year.

Depending upon the anticipated size of my students' portfolios, they are maintained in either a folder or box. My students' portfolios typically contain not only their work but assessment records for selected items such as personal reflection sheets and rubrics that evaluate the chosen pieces.

I like to use portfolios because they are not only folders of student products and processes but also valuable assessment tools. They can effectively demonstrate students' progress in a limited way such as within an assignment itself, or they can reveal comprehensive growth by showing student work from the beginning to the end of the school year or term. For example, with some writing assignments, I ask my students to include their rough drafts, edited copies, and final copies, thus revealing the steps each went through in completing an assignment.

While I use portfolios for assessment purposes, I have noted that students look at their portfolios for feedback on ways to improve their work. In this way, my students acquire a sense of ownership of their ongoing learning processes. Other forms of assessment often fail to accomplish this important form of reflection.

In my Multiple Intelligences classroom, I try to insure that portfolios incorporate evidence of work in all seven intelligences. Over the years I have included the following portfolio entries. This list might suggest a range of possibilities for your students' portfolios as well.

- All forms of written work including drafts, peer-edited versions, teacher-edited versions, final copies. (e.g. creative writing, research papers, poetry, and reports)

- Recipes, directions, plans for completing work

- Math assignments, including calculations and problem-solving

- Paintings, drawings, and designs

- Charts, graphs, diagrams

- Photographs of sculptures, constructions, sewing, etc.

- Musical scores

- Audiotapes of musical performances

- Videotapes of plays, dances, interviews, presentations

- Learning logs

- Personal reflection sheets

- Rubrics and other evaluation forms

- Project contracts

- Statements of personal goals

- Checklists for classroom tasks

- Research notes

- Computer-generated work (spreadsheets, databases, graphics, etc.)

- Peer or parent feedback forms

Student Reflection Sheets

One of the most important aspects of assessment is to teach students how to assess their own work. Even very young students can develop reflective skills when asked to do so. Reflection helps students to internalize their own inner editors, to identify the strengths and weaknesses of their work, and to manage their individual learning. I have used the following two forms, the Personal Reflection Sheet and the Self-Assessment Sheet, with my students when I wanted them to reflect on work that is to be included in their portfolios, or when I wanted them to evaluate the quality of a specific assignment.

Personal Reflection Sheet
(Use with work to be included in your portfolio.)

Name _____   Date _____

Title of piece _____

Description of piece: _____
_____
_____

What did you learn from working on this assignment? _____
_____
_____

What did you learn about yourself from working on this piece? _____
_____
_____

What could be done to enhance your work?_____
_____
_____

What challenges or problems did you encounter? _____
_____
_____

Does this work meet the specified criteria? How or why not?_____
_____
_____

In what ways does this work encourage you to pursue this area further?_____
_____
_____

STUDENT SELF-ASSESSMENT

(Use to assess your work on designated assignments.)

Name _____ Date _____

Assignment _____

1. What was your goal? _____
   _____

2. How well did you accomplish your goal? _____
   _____
   _____

3. What is the best part of your work on this assignment? _____
   _____
   _____

5. What parts may need improvement? _____
   _____
   _____

6. What was your least favorite activity when working on this assignment? _____
   _____
   _____

7. What did you learn about yourself while working on this? _____
   _____
   _____

8. If you did the assignment over, how would it be different? _____
   _____
   _____

9. How does this assignment connect with other work in this class or in others?
   _____
   _____

10. What score or grade do you think this work deserves? Why? _____
    _____

Peer-Assessment: The Appreciation Sandwich

After class presentations, I always invite my students to critique each other. Students can be taught to provide constructive feedback with tact and diplomacy. In my classroom, feedback is built into each day's activities. At the completion of center-time, students volunteer to share the products they created that day. Individuals and groups informally share their reading, writing, art work, skits, models, and songs. After the sharing is completed, the rest of the class comments upon strong and weak points in the various presentations.

A second and more formal opportunity for feedback occurs when students present their independent projects. Each student receives five to ten minutes of constructive criticism, based upon the criteria established for that assignment from both myself and other students.

One technique I teach my students to use in critiquing each other is the "Appreciation Sandwich." In an "Appreciation Sandwich" a critical comment is sandwiched between two positive comments. For example, if one of my students, Krisiti, were studying Arabian horses, I might give her the following Appreciation Sandwich about her presentation:

"Kristi, I enjoyed your presentation on Arabian horses. It was an interesting topic for me because I never knew how Arabians were different from other horses. Your eye contact needs work. You kept looking down at the floor and I wanted you to look up at me. Your visuals were great; in particular, the one chart that compared Arabians to other horses helped me understand the differences between varieties of horses."

Human nature being as it is, Kristi will remember the critical comment, but she will also, hopefully, remember the positive input as well.

During my years of teaching, I have observed that "Appreciation Sandwiches" are as effective as any other form of assessment in encouraging change in student work. Consistently, students respond to and follow through with each other's recommendations as well as continue to build upon their identified strengths.

Long-Term Student Project Assessment

Since my students are required to do eight major projects during each school year, I wanted to determine whether the quality of student projects improved over time. I became curious about whether students consistently relied upon one or two modes to communicate information, whether their research skills improved, and whether their projects grew more sophisticated.

To secure such information, I developed the following rubric. On cardstock, I photocopy one rubric per student and use it as one assessment device for monthly project presentations. The cardstock is sturdy enough to last the entire school year, and I maintain these student records in my filing cabinet for easy retrieval. Some years, I have also made copies of the rubric for students to use themselves so that they can track their progress with projects over the course of the school year as well.

Project Evaluation Sheet

Name: _____

— P R O J E C T S —

Criteria Topic:	1	2	3	4	5	6	7	8	Comments
Began with effective introduction									
Was well organized									
Did effective research									
Understood major concepts									
Provided good supporting data									
Offered good examples & elaboration of content									
Had a strong closing									
Used effective presentation skills									
Included visual aids									
Included music									
Included a kinesthetic component									
Included interpersonal elements									
Included intrapersonal elements									
Included logical-mathematical components									
Included effective linguistic components									

A Multiple Intelligences Report Card

Not only have some of my daily assessment processes changed, but so has my report card. Once I started my MI classroom model, I soon realized that the traditional report card failed to capture the work my students were actually doing. To better reflect our classroom efforts, I created the following report card. This report attempts to portray the developmental level of each student in all seven intelligences through a bar graph format. I use a different color for each of the four marking periods, and I attempt to show whether a student is developmentally at a novice, apprentice, practitioner, or scholar level for each criterion.

In the event that a student does not progress within an area between marking periods, I draw a vertical line to represent the static nature of that criterion. Most students, however, continue to grow in each of the following areas over the course of a school year. Sometimes, I make brief narrative comments below each bar if appropriate. You'll also note a special section at the end for follow-up suggestions. Here I make recommendations about what parents might do to enhance the strengths of their child as well as to remediate any apparent weaknesses.

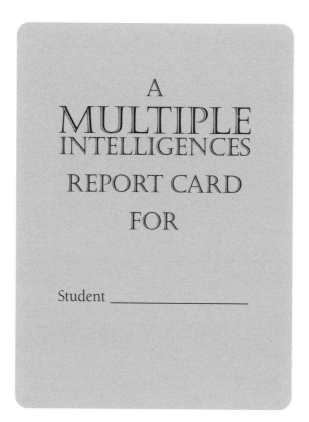

A
MULTIPLE
INTELLIGENCES
REPORT CARD
FOR

Student _____

Multiple Intelligences Report Card with Developmental Indicators

Name _____

	Novice	Apprentice	Practitioner	Scholar

Reading
(Linguistic Intelligence)

Writing & Spelling
(Linguistic Intelligence)

Math & Science
(Logical-Mathematical Intelligence)

Visual Arts
(Visual-Spatial Intelligence)

Movement Activities
(Bodily-Kinesthetic Intelligence)

Building Activities
(Bodily-Kinesthetic Intelligence)

Music Skills
(Musical Intelligence)

Group Work
(Interpersonal Intelligence)

Reflective Thinking
(Intrapersonal Intelligence)

Research
(Project Preparation Skills)

Presentations
(Project Demonstration Skills)

Novice ....recognizes concepts, begins to develop skills
Apprentice.........acquires increasingly complex skills through guided practice
Practitioner ......works independently and accurately with knowledge and skills
Scholar...............demonstrates mastery of concepts and practices, applies in new settings

(Colored bars demonstrate beginning points in each area as well as extent of progress at this time. The longer the line, the greater the improvement. New colors represent new grading periods.)

PART V: TEACHING MI LESSONS

Whenever I do workshops for teachers on the topic of The Multiple Intelligences, I am frequently asked, "Do you have lesson plans already prepared that you could share with me?" Now I can say "yes" because this section of the Handbook is filled with lessons from a variety of subject areas. The contents of this section begin with Lesson #2 since the first on teaching students about the Multiple Intelligences was included in Part II :

Part V Contents:

These lessons can be taught to students in a number of ways. The students might work in groups at learning centers, or the class may be organized with a whole-group, direct instruction format. The timeframe can vary: some lessons may be completed in one hour or one day, or spread across a week or month. The lessons presented here may also serve as parts of larger units and broad themes. For example, a lesson on Christopher Columbus could be integrated into a unit on the Age of Exploration or early American history with the theme of Discoveries.

In addition, lesson sections can be divided into dozens of individual MI activities for the classroom. The teacher should determine what to teach when. The sequence of activities within the lessons as presented here does not dictate the order in which they might be taught in the classroom. For example, even though the lessons all begin with linguistic activities, the teacher may want to begin with the kinesthetic or visual activities. Teachers should feel free to use any sequence appropriate.

Finally, it is not essential to teach every lesson in seven ways. Teachers are encouraged to pick and choose activities that fit their particular lessons on any given day. However, it is important to provide opportunities for students to learn in each of the seven intelligences at least some time during each major unit of study.

LESSON #2:   ADJECTIVES

Subject Area:	Language Arts
Main Concept:	Correct use of modifiers
Principle To Be Taught:	Written or oral language is enhanced with descriptive words
Unit:	Parts of speech
Previous Lesson:	Verbs
Following Lesson:	Adverbs
Grade level:	3-8
Materials Needed:	Graph paper
	Large blank cards
	Paper and colored markers
	5 to 8 large sheets of butcher paper
	Written text with several adjectives for assessment activity

Linguistic Activity:

On the blackboard, the teacher lists several adjectives. Students write phrases or sentences using these modifiers on a topic suggested by the teacher or by students.

Younger students might be given a written story with blanks where the adjectives should be written. The students' task would be to fill in the blanks with adjectives from a list on the chalkboard or with their own words.

Logical-Mathematical Activity:

Students can count the number of adjectives as well as nouns and verbs in a given piece of text. It might be interesting to ask an expert writer if there are standard ratios of parts of speech. (Remember the assumption of this lesson is that students have previously studied nouns and verbs.) A sample chart is provided for quantifying the parts of speech.

	# of nouns	# of verbs	# of adjectives
paragraph #1			
paragraph #2			
paragraph #3			
paragraph #4			
paragraph #5			
paragraph #6			

Next, students might compare the numbers of each part of speech by drawing a bar graph or pie chart. This can be done on graph paper or on the computer. A sample graph is demonstrated below:

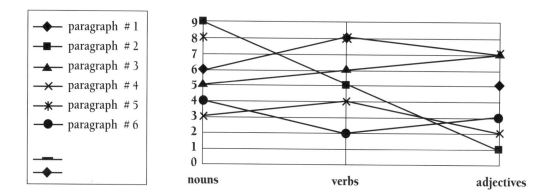

Kinesthetic Activity:

For this activity, the teacher will need to write several sentences with one word per large blank card ahead of class. When class begins, distribute several blank cards to each student. Ask for volunteers to stand in front of the class with the word cards that you have prepared. Each volunteer should have one card and the group should form a sentence to display for the class. The students who are seated write adjectives on their word cards that are appropriate for the displayed sentence. Students raise their hands and when called on, move to the front of the class inserting their adjectives into the sentence. Other students may also move up to the front, tap an "adjective" on the shoulder and replace it with a new one. The same process could be adapted for individual student work if students use smaller word cards at their desks with teacher- or textbook-provided sentences.

Visual-Spatial Activity:

Students should be provided with drawing paper and crayons or markers. The teacher then gives *adjective instructions* such as the following.

- Draw a bold, red, squiggley line.
- Draw a small, multi-colored, rectangular box.
- Draw a sparse, bare, wispy tree.

After completing the drawings, the teacher could ask the students to write the adjectives next to each object they described.

Musical Activity:

Identify a song that students know but change the adjectives. *Mary had a little lamb…its fleece was white as snow* would work well with young children. Teachers can call on different students to vocally insert a new modifier at the appropriate time.

Interpersonal Activity:

Working in groups of four or five, students choose a mascot, select four or five adjectives to describe that mascot, and then illustrate the mascot on butcher paper. Each student in the group is responsible for illustrating one characteristic based upon the adjective he or she selected.

For example, one group might choose *Aliens* as their mascot and become the *green, slimy, toothy, ugly, smiley aliens.* They would then draw their green, slimy, toothy, ugly, smiley alien, with each student coloring in the part suggested by his or her chosen adjective.

Next, each picture is held up for the class to see. Students attempt to guess the five modifiers in each team mascot.

Intrapersonal Activity:

To increase intrapersonal awareness, students make individual lists of adjectives to describe themselves such or write narrative descriptions of themselves.

To extend the lesson one step further, each student might be asked to explain why he/she has chosen such adjectives. For example: *I am a sad person. The reason I am sad is because my dog died last week and I miss her. I am also a responsible person. The reason I am responsible is because I like to do my chores without anyone asking me to.*

Assessment:

With a written selection of text, students use a colored marker to underline all adjectives. They then trade papers with a partner and correct each other's paper with a different colored marker.

LESSON #3   MAGNETISM

Subject Area:	Science
Main Concept:	Forces in nature
Principle To Be Taught:	Magnetic fields are comprised of attraction and repulsion forces
Unit:	Physical science: electricity and magnetism
Previous Lesson:	Gravitational fields
Following Lesson:	Electric fields
Grade level:	3-10
Materials Needed:	Printed material with information on magnets and magnetism
	Magnets of varying sizes and shapes
	Paper clips, pins, nails
	Iron filings
	One or more small postal scales
	Percussion instruments
	Optional: small boxes, wire, compasses

Linguistic Activity:

In a science text encyclopedia, or library book, students read about magnets and magnetism. Most sources give narrative descriptions and illustrations of the magnetic fields of a variety of magnets. After reading the selection, students might answer the following questions:

  • How are magnets made?
  • How do magnets work?
  • What causes magnetism?
  • How are magnets of different shapes used?

Logical-Mathematical Activity:

Working with magnets of different sizes and shapes, students pick up paper clips or other magnetic objects. They can be asked to count how many clips each magnet holds and record their findings. For variety, suggest that students weigh the clips on small postal scales and then compare the weights. Students might also explore pins, nails, or other objects to determine whether magnetic strength varies depending upon the objects being attracted.

Kinesthetic Activity:

Ask students to experiment with magnets by just "playing" with them in order to observe their properties and strengths. Then ask students to observe in a more deliberate manner which objects are magnetic.

One excellent activity suggested in many science books involves students making their own electromagnets to see the magnetic effects of electricity. To make an electromagnet, teachers can demonstrate how to wrap about 10 turns of wire around a small box, forming a coil. Next strip the insulation from the ends of the wire and connect the wires to the terminals of a dry cell battery. Place a compass inside the box and turn the box so that the compass needle lines up with the wire. Observe how the compass needle moves.

By reversing the wires on the terminals or adding more turns to the coil, further effects can be observed. If the ends of the wire are switched back and forth between the terminals at just the right speed, the needle on the compass can actually be made to spin. Students can be asked to explain the various phenomena they observe.

Visual-Spatial Activity:

Working in small groups, students can map the field of a bar magnet by placing an iron magnet under a sheet of white paper and sprinkling iron filings on the paper. When the paper is gently tapped, the filings will flow into a very distinct pattern radiating away from the magnetic poles. Students can be asked to draw similar patterns with charcoal or pencil, and to explain why this happens.

For variation, students can place two bar magnets under the paper and observe different patterns in the filings, depending upon whether the poles of the two magnets are attracting or repelling each other. These patterns can also be drawn and the poles of the magnet identified: N and N if the poles are alike, N and S if they are different.

Musical Activity:

In small groups, provide students with drums, tambourines, rhythm sticks, or other percussion instruments. Ask them to create an attracting and repelling melody. Attracting melodies might have two instruments (or two groups of instruments) alternating their sounds. Repelling melodies might play simultaneously. Or, attracting rhythms might include an echo (one student beats a rhythm, others imitate it) while repelling rhythms are dissimilar.

Interpersonal Activity:

Ask students to stand in pairs with arms crossed on their chests to pantomime magnets and their fields. The teacher can call out directions, which might include:

> You are both magnets.
>
> Your arms are your positive pole, your back is your negative pole.
>
> The magnetism is turned off until I say "on."
>
> Stand about three feet apart facing each other...*On..........Off.*
>
> One person turn halfway around so you are front to back...*On.....Off.*
>
> The other person turns so that you are back to back...*On..........Off.*

Such directions can continue until students understand the concept. Variation can be added with *high-low, fast-slow, smooth-jerky, big-small,* and other elements of movement. The addition of music can turn the activity from creative-magnetic movement into a dance of magnets.

Intrapersonal Activity:

Ask students to reflect individually in their journals on "magnetic" phenomena in their lives. Provide starter sentences as follows:

> I am attracted to _____.
>
> I am repelled by _____.
>
> I am attracted to _____.
>
> I am repelled by _____.
>
> I am attracted to _____.
>
> I am repelled by _____.
>
> I am attracted to _____.
>
> I am repelled by _____.

Assessment:

To demonstrate their understanding of magnetism as a force in nature, provide students with magnets, metal filings, and other magnetic and non-magnetic objects; have them create their own experiment to demonstrate principles of magnetism. They can work individually or in small groups to demonstrate what is happening as well as explain *why* the phenomena occurs.

LESSON #4:   ADDING FRACTIONS

Subject Area:	Math
Main Concept:	Mathematics involves numbers and parts of numbers
Principle To Be Taught:	Parts of a whole can be combined
Unit:	Fractions
Previous Lesson:	Common denominators
Following Lesson:	Subtracting fractions
Grade level:	4-6
Materials Needed:	Copies of the fraction stories (in the linguistic activity)
	Sheets of music
	Beans or other manipulatives
	One piece of cardstock per student

 ## Linguistic Activity:

Provide copies of the following two fraction stories to students. Ask them to illustrate the images described in the stories.

Maria suddenly found herself in the land of fractions. There was one-half of a house, two-thirds of a mountain, one-fourth of a tree. Even the animals were fractional. She saw a dog with only three-fourths of its legs and an elephant with four-fifths of a trunk. The weirdest thing was a bird with only half its wings, one wing that is, and it kept flying around in circles.

The old train crept up the mountain. It was 204 miles to the top. After three hours it passed the halfway marker so the engineer knew they were one-half of the way to the top. But now the mountain was steeper and the train slowed even more. After another three hours it was halfway from that last marker to the top. How far would that be?

Once students have read and illustrated the above two samples, ask them to create their own fraction word problems or stories.

 ## Logical-Mathematical Activity:

Ask students to pretend that they are math textbook authors and that they must create formulas in their own words for adding fractions while also providing examples of fractions being added according to their formulas.

Kinesthetic Activity:

Many manipulatives such as blocks, counters, and beans can be used for fractions. In the absence of manipulatives, the teacher or students can make simple sets of fractions from paper cut into pizza-like shapes.

A sample activity would be to give each student 24 beans. Ask them to divide the beans in half, and divide one of those halves in half again. Students should now have three piles, one of 12 and two of six. Explain that each of the two smaller piles represents one-fourth of the total pile. If students add one-fourth plus one-fourth they will have ____ beans, which is the same as what fraction of the total?

An excellent set of manipulatives for working with fractions is called DIVIO, available from Joyfullearning, P.O. Box 1407, Ferndale, WA, 98248.

Visual-Spatial Activity:

Students can make Fraction Strips out of cardstock. Each student should cut out five strips, about two inches by twelve inches as shown:

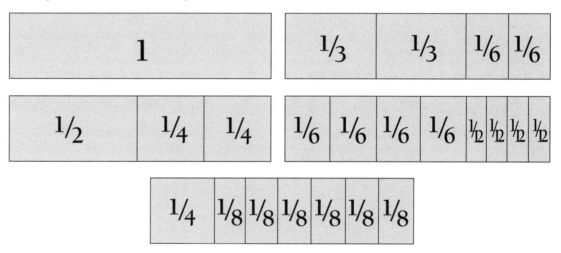

After labeling the parts of each strip, students can be directed to cut them into their fractional parts. Pieces should be labeled with student names on the back and kept in an envelope so they don't get lost. [Fraction Strip Games are described under the following Interpersonal Activity]

Musical Activity:

Studying fractions offers a perfect time to learn to read music. Provide students with sheets of music. Show them quarter notes, half notes, and whole notes. Once they have learned these three symbols, they can progress to making music with clapping or with rhythm sticks. The teacher or a student can clap out a steady rhythm (whole notes), with the class echoing the leader. Then clap out double time (half notes) and quadruple time (quarter notes).

Interpersonal Activity:

Games for two to four players using the fraction strips from the preceding visual-spatial activity are described below:

MAKE A WHOLE
1. Players mix their fractional parts into one pile.
2. Each player takes out one fractional part per turn until all the parts are gone.
3. Each player tries to make as many whole "ones" as possible by placing pieces on the uncut strip.

PAIRS
1. Players work in pairs, mixing their cards into one pile.
2. Set a time limit (2, 3, or 4 minutes).
3. Teams put together as many halves as possible within the time limit.

TAKE TEN
1. Players work in groups of three or four.
2. Each player selects ten fraction parts and puts them into a group pile.
3. As a group, the players then try to make as many whole "ones" as possible.

Intrapersonal Activity:

Ask students to write their favorite activities on the back of each fraction strip piece e.g. playing video games, reading, listening to music, playing football, talking on the telephone, eating ice cream, etc. Then each student fits his or her pieces together to make one full day of activities. "One whole day" can only hold only so many "parts."

Assessment:

Working individually or in pairs, students mix all their fraction strips into one pile. They demonstrate their understanding of fractions by reassembling all five (or ten if they are working in pairs) of their strips into wholes. To increase the challenge, make this a timed activity. To add variety, the pieces can all be placed face-down so that students have to reassemble the parts visually. It is important for teacher and students to realize that there is more than one correct method of completing this task.

LESSON #5:	CHRISTOPHER COLUMBUS

Subject Area:	Social Studies
Main Concept:	Exploration
Principle To Be Taught:	Explorations affect native cultures
Unit:	Early American history
Previous Lesson:	Americans before Columbus
Following Lesson:	Magellan, other explorers
Grade level:	3-8
Materials Needed:	Contrasting written accounts of Christopher Columbus
	Butcher paper
	World map and opaque projector
	Caribbean and European music
	(See Musical Activity)

 ## Linguistic Activity:

Many social studies textbooks describe the voyages of Columbus, but usually from one point of view. An interesting resource for teachers that offers an alternative perspective on Columbus's arrival in the Americas is *A People's History of the United States* by Howard Zinn. Students may benefit from realizing that Columbus was not only a great explorer, he was also a ruthless conqueror who invaded the land of the Arawaks and nearly destroyed their culture. Students might read contrasting accounts of Columbus's life, and then attempt to reconcile them. Why is he generally portrayed as a hero? What contributions did he make? How might things have been different without him? What impact did his actions have on American Indians?

 ## Logical-Mathematical Activity:

Studying Columbus's journey across the Atlantic provides students with opportunities to study maps and scales as well as math problems addressing "distance = rate x time." Teachers may want to provide students with the following data:

- Columbus traveled over 4,000 miles.
- It took him 36 days to cross the Atlantic on the outward journey and 58 days to return.
- His ship was about 80 feet long and carried only 40 men.
- Modern ocean-going ships are often over 1,000 feet long and can carry over 3,000 passengers.

Such facts provide ample material for mathematical problem-solving. Some sample problems for students to solve might include:

- If Columbus left the Canary Islands on August 12, 1492 and landed in the Bahamas on October 12, how many days was he at sea?

- If the Santa Maria traveled 4,286 miles in 36 days, what was the average number of miles the ship traveled per day?

- If Columbus started out with 90 men and 7 died on the trip west, 15 stayed in the Bahamas, 9 Arawaks were loaded onto the ships before heading east, 19 were lost in a storm on the return voyage, and 12 deserted in the Azores, how many men returned to Portugal with him?

- If the Santa Maria were 80 feet long, the Pinta were 72 feet long, and the Nina were 67 feet long, and they were tied up bow to stern on a dock, how long would the dock have to be?

- If a 1,027-foot-long modern ocean liner were tied up next to Columbus's three ships, how much longer would it be than the combined length of the Pinta, the Nina, and the Santa Maria?

Kinesthetic Activity:

Ask students to dramatize Columbus's arrival in the Caribbean. Have students assume the roles of Columbus, his companions, and the Arawak people who greeted them.

Visual-Spatial Activity:

Students can create a large map of the world as a classroom mural. The map can be made from pieces of butcher paper taped together. The easiest way to outline such a map is to tack the paper onto the wall and use an overhead or opaque projector to project a map of the world onto the butcher paper. Either students or the teacher can trace the outlines of the continents onto the paper.

Students can color in whatever features the teacher selects: mountain ranges, countries, rivers, cities, locations of important historical events, homelands of students in the class or their ancestors, as well as the voyage of Columbus. The map can serve as a working document with additional features added as new units are undertaken.

Musical Activity:

Students can listen to period music from the two cultures. Most European music in the late fifteenth and early sixteenth centuries was primarily religious. Gregorian chant was still prevalent, madrigals were emerging, and compositions featuring stringed instruments such as the lute were popular. Recordings of such music are readily available. One early madrigal composer was Palestrina.

The music of the Caribbean in the fifteenth and sixteenth centuries is more uncertain. Probably, however, some of the steel drum music being recorded today is reminiscent of that time and place.

Ask students to listen to the musical selections and reflect upon the following questions:

- What does each piece of music make you think about?

- What kinds of instruments are used?

- What images of the various cultures are provoked when you listen to the different selections? How might you determine whether such impressions are accurate?

- What moods do the different kinds of music evoke?

Interpersonal Activity:

Working in groups of four to six, students can discuss a plan for peacefully blending two cultures. They could address a hypothetical situation such as two fictional cultures, any two contemporary cultures, or the American Indian and European cultures under consideration.

Some questions the groups might consider include:

- Should one culture take the lead in establishing a blended culture?

- Should the new culture be a mixture of two separate cultures or a true blend?

- What separate characteristics of each culture should be retained?

- What common qualities or features should a new blended culture develop?

- What should each culture be willing to sacrifice?

- How should a form of governance be established?

- How might such blending occur without risking dictatorship?

- Who has the right to decide which elements of which culture should be retained and which discarded?

Intrapersonal Activity:

Students respond in writing to the question: If you were Christopher Columbus or the Chief of the Arawak people, how would you have handled the arrival of the Europeans?

Assessment:

Students might demonstrate their understanding of the complex issues involved in the arrival of Columbus in America by drawing parallels with two current cultures, subcultures, groups, or even individuals confronting each other today. Students might write or role play a new family moving into a neighborhood, a new student arriving at a school, or a contemporary international problem. They should address the similarities and differences with Columbus arriving in the West Indies. They should also anticipate how the relationships might unfold.

LESSON #6:   WHALES

Subject Area:	Science
Main Concept:	Diverse habitats
Principle To Be Taught:	Marine mammals live in water, but need to breathe air
Unit:	Mammals
Previous Lesson:	Land mammals
Following Lesson:	Dolphins, porpoises, seals, etc.
Grade level:	K-8
Materials Needed:	Library materials on whales
	Butcher paper and newspaper
	Song by Judy Collins called "Whales and Nightingales" or tapes or CD's of whale songs
	Large pieces of colored chalk
	Book-making supplies

Linguistic Activity:

Many books about whales and other aquatic mammals can be found in most school libraries. Depending upon reading levels, students can survey reference books on whales and write brief reports about a variety of whales and how they live and breathe in the ocean. For poor readers, the teacher might provide a short lecture with visuals to explain how whales live. Next, students might draw a whale, labeling its parts, and explaining in both narrative and pictorial form how whales live and breathe.

Logical-Mathematical Activity:

Students can quantitatively explore the lives of whales. Fascinating information is available about their size (blue whales grow up to 100 feet), their weight, the amount of food they must eat, the temperature of water in the ocean where whales live, the depths they swim to, and the lengths of time they can stay under water. Students might create charts comparing and contrasting varieties of whales.

Another logical-mathematical activity is to create story problems with whale facts. Problems can range from simple arithmetic to more complex problem-solving, as the following examples demonstrate:

- If five whales meet three whales, how many whales are there?

- If a whale eats 500 pounds of krill in a day, how much will it eat in a week?

- If the temperature of the ocean on the surface is 52° F., and drops 5° every 75 feet, what will the temperature be if a humpback whale dives to 1,275 feet?

- Why do beached whales die, when they can still breathe air? (The answer has to do with gravity, lack of buoyancy, pressure on the lungs.)

Kinesthetic Activity:

Many games can be adapted for a whale theme. "Whales in the Ocean" is one option that can be played outdoors or in the gym. Students line up on one end of the gym or playground. One person is selected as a whale hunter by the teacher. Each student chooses one of four types of whales (e.g. sperm, humpback, orca, finback). The whale hunter calls out the four types randomly. Students whose whale type has been chosen run to the opposite end of the play field trying to avoid the whale hunter, who tries to tag them. If students are tagged, they too become whale hunters. If the original whale hunter calls out "Whales in the Ocean," everyone runs. The last student tagged becomes the new whale hunter, and the game begins again.

An indoor classroom activity might be the building of a giant whale to hang in the room or hallway. One class made a 25-foot orca by pasting together giant sheets of butcher paper, tracing the whale, cutting out two matching pieces, painting them black and white to look like an orca, gluing or stapling the edges together, and then stuffing the inside with crumpled newspaper. It hung dramatically in the school library for the rest of the year.

Visual-Spatial Activity:

To really "see" the size of a giant blue whale, students can draw one on a paved surface such as a playground, parking lot, or driveway of the school. Using chalk which washes out with the first rain, a class can quickly rough out and then fill in a large (100 feet) blue whale. Various parts such as the dorsal fin, blowhole, and baleen can be drawn and labeled. One such blue whale made by a second grade class was recently featured on the front page of the local newspaper.

For those less inclined to undertake such a project, students can draw to scale the sizes of various whales on individual charts. Most encyclopedias or books about whales provide examples of such charts.

Musical Activity:

Several tapes and CDs are available with the songs of humpback whales. Some are pure whale sounds, others such as Judy Collin's "Whales and Nightingales" combine whale songs with instrumental music.

Students can analyze the music looking for specific sounds or patterns. They might listen to it more informally, or the teacher might play it as background music during other classroom activities.

Interpersonal Activity:

Combining art, research, and writing skills, students in groups of four or five can make books about whales. The groups divide up the tasks for book-making by assigning roles such as researcher, writer, illustrator, layout and binding person, and cover designer. This project will probably require one to two weeks of time as students plan, prepare, and construct their group whale books.

Intrapersonal Activity:

Students write or dictate their own *If I were a whale I would be a _____* (kind of whale) story. They should choose a favorite type of whale and write about why they made such a choice. They should address some of the following questions:

- About how long are you?

- About how much do you weigh?

- What do you eat?

- What do you look like?

- Where do you live or travel?

- How long can you stay under water?

- What is the greatest danger to you?

- How would you feel about living in captivity and being in shows?

- What is unique about the way you live?

- How are you similar to or different from other kinds of whales?

- What are your greatest fears and concerns?

Assessment:

The interpersonal or intrapersonal activities could be used for assessment.

LESSON #7:   BEN FRANKLIN

Subject Area:	Social Studies
Main Concept:	Democracy
Principle To Be Taught:	Freedom of speech is a fundamental American right
Unit:	Colonial America
Previous Lesson:	Thomas Jefferson
Following Lesson:	Causes of American Revolution
Grade level:	4-9
Materials Needed:	Ben Franklin library materials
	Sample political cartoons
	Journal materials
Field Trip Possibility:	To a printing company or local newspaper

Linguistic Activity:

Original source materials are not only more relevant to researchers but are often more interesting to teachers and students than textbooks. Teachers might want to contact local public libraries to find copies of Ben Franklin's original writings and use these with students as classroom "texts." Some specific titles include: *Sayings of Poor Richard*, copies of his "Pennsylvania Gazette," and his *Autobiography*.

It would be interesting for students to learn that Ben Franklin was not only a statesman and outspoken advocate for democracy but also a successful inventor, writer, political cartoonist, publisher, scientist, diplomat, and gardener. All of his activities, in fact, his life itself, was a model for freedom of expression, which manifests itself in the form of government Franklin helped to shape and believed in so deeply, as well as in his publications which promoted free speech.

Logical-Mathematical Activity:

Ben Franklin was a scientist, inventing many things such as a wood stove, bifocal glasses, and the lightning rod. He also discovered electricity. To invent something, he first determined what was needed.

Students can be asked to become inventors by thinking of a need and creating something to fill that need. This could be something fantastic such as a homework machine or an automatic diaper changer, or something real such as an ozone replacer, or new kind of cereal container. In small groups, students should follow these steps:

Inventing something useful:

1. Identify needs of one's peers or society in general.

2. Select one or two needs for the group to address.

3. Brainstorm a list of possible inventions.

4. Select one invention and one need to work on.

5. Create two or more possible designs.

6. Evaluate the designs and select the best one.

7. Design an invention on paper, with clay, or other materials.

8. If possible, build a model or prototype.

9. Share the invention with others.

One important principle in this lesson is brainstorming. Indirectly, it relates to the concept of free speech. As students prepare for this activity, remind them of the rules of brainstorming:

1. Be freewheeling and creative. Anything goes!

2. Don't criticize others' ideas.

3. Write down *everything* that is suggested.

 ## Kinesthetic Activity:

Ben was an outspoken advocate for freedom of the press. When he was young, he acquired a printing press and soon published a newspaper. He felt that it was vital to speak up and write about important political issues. The press was Ben Franklin's instrument for sharing his ideas and opinions.

If possible, it would be valuable to arrange a field trip for students to explore how newspapers and printing presses work. Visits to local newspapers, printing companies, or local museums with old presses can show students the mechanics of mass production of the written word.

After or instead of a field trip, students might do some of their own printing. Young students can make rubber stamps or create block or potato prints. Older ones may want to work with word processing software and a printer to create titles or headlines for class newspaper. (see Interpersonal Activity on next page.)

Visual-Spatial Activity:

Ben Franklin often included political cartoons in the papers he printed. Students can also draw their own political cartoons poking fun at things in the school or community which they find unjust or unnecessary. One rule for their political cartoons is that they cannot poke fun at another person (unless perhaps he or she is a national figure). Political cartoons from local newspapers could be brought in as examples.

Some sample ideas might include showing a child in a phone booth unable to reach the phone, trying to open plastic wrapping on food without a sharp knife, carrying big boom boxes, or taking home too much homework.

Musical Activity:

Individually, students write facts they have learned about Ben Franklin, one per note card. On the blackboard, the teacher writes the refrain included below. The students practice saying or "singing" the refrain. They then take turns reading their cards. After two to four cards are read, the whole group joins in with the refrain. Other cards are read, followed by the refrain, and so on.

Boogie Woogie Ben
With just a quill pen
Helped make America free
For you and you and me.

Interpersonal Activity:

Working either in groups or as a whole class, students create their own newspaper with a title including a term such as Gazette, Examiner, Journal, Herald, Inquirer, or Times. The derivation of such terms could be discussed when choosing the titles as well as the fact that the purpose of the newspaper is to "inquire" about or "examine" what is happening or what people think, and to disperse this information. Students should understand that the newspaper is a means of sharing diverse perspectives in a democratic society.

Students can be assigned reporters' roles for their newspaper work. It is often effective to have two students work together on such topics as:

School news	World news
Advertising	Artwork
Cartoons	Foreign language column
Weather	TV reviews
Editorials	Book reviews
Sports	Movie reviews
Question-and-Answer Columns	(like those of Dear Abby)

Intrapersonal Activity:

Ben Franklin faithfully kept a diary. Using Ben as a role model, students could begin their own journal or diary. Classroom journals can be used in a variety of ways:

- as a diary which is kept confidential or shared with only the teacher
- as a log to document daily learning experiences
- for creative writing: ongoing stories, poems, narratives
- for dictation: teacher dictates a sentence or two each day for writing practice
- as a teacher/student dialog in which the teacher responds to student writing
- as a student/ student dialog in which students are paired up and respond to each other's writing
- for a short, teacher-designed, daily writing assignment
- to record favorite quotes or passages from books
- a combination of any of the above

Assessment:

A culminating essay could measure student learning about Ben Franklin. The essay might include information about Ben's life, his scientific, journalistic, and political work, and what each student considers to be his most significant contributions, and why.

A visual assessment tool might require that students make a collage of Ben Franklin's life, depicting the same categories as the essay. The collage could include original drawings, photocopies, magazine pictures, or combinations of illustrations and text.

LESSON #8:   THE STORY ABOUT PING

Subject Area:	Language Arts
Main Concept:	Adventures in fiction can reflect real life
Principle To Be Taught:	The same emotions are universally experienced
Unit:	China
Previous Lesson:	Rivers of China
Following Lesson:	People who live in boats
Grade level:	K-4
Materials Needed:	A copy of *The Story about Ping* by Marjorie Flack
	Materials to make a game board such as markers, butcher paper or card stock, dice
	Chinese music or classroom musical instruments

 ## Linguistic Activity:

Teachers can read The Story about Ping or ask that students read it themselves. Most second graders will be capable of reading it independently. As a follow-up, students might orally compose their own stories about animals or people getting lost and their subsequent adventures. Sitting in a circle, one student begins with an opening sentence, and others add onto it in turn.

 ## Logical-Mathematical Activity:

In the story Ping had many relatives. Every evening when it was time to return to the boat where Ping lived, the ducks were all counted. Such story contents suggest numerous counting activities.

Teachers might ask students:

What are some of the things that we keep track of by counting?

What do we do when the count comes up short?

How did counting get started in the first place?

In addition, students could solve math problems derived from the story:

• If 17 ducks got off the boat in the morning and only 12 returned in the evening, how many ducks were left behind?

- If there were 12 ducks and only half of them got off the boat, how many remained on the boat?

- If Ping had 9 brothers and 13 sisters, how many ducklings were in his family? (Don't forget to count Ping.)

- If there were 4 families of ducks and 6 ducks in each family, how many ducks would there be altogether?

- If one family had 23 ducks and another family had 32 ducks, which would be the larger family? By how many?

- If a duck ran away from its family to live in the wild, what would be some of the main problems it would encounter?

- If someone gave you 25 ducks and you were allowed to keep only one, how would you decide which one to keep and what would you do with the others?

Kinesthetic Activity:

There are several kinesthetic options appropriate for this story. I have listed five below:

1. It might be possible to have a pet duck visit the classroom. Students could observe its physical features and behavior, hold it, feed it, and learn how to care for it.

2. A field trip might be arranged to a farm, zoo, or wildlife refuge to observe ducks.

3. Students might make ducks out of clay since this is a shape that even young children can fashion with success.

4. The class might make a duck pinata from paper mache and put Chinese rice candies or fortune cookies inside.

5. During recess or P.E. students might play the game "Duck, Duck, Goose," a circle game much like "Drop the Handkerchief." To play, all students stand in a circle facing inward. One student (it) runs around the outside of the circle saying, "I had a little duck and it didn't bite you, and it didn't bite you, and it didn't bite you, but it did bite YOU!" Then "it" tags a student on the back who races "it" around the circle to see who can be the first to reach the empty space left by the tagged child.

Visual-Spatial Activity:

Students can draw a map of Ping's adventures on the Yangtze River as follows:
1. Begin by drawing, coloring, or painting a river winding across the page.

2. Add boats, wild animals, other people, and experiences of the duck.

3. Fill in the background with grass, trees, houses, mountains, etc.

Musical Activity:

The story of Peter and the Wolf emerged from Prokofiev's symphonic work. Why not reverse the process and put a story to music? This could be done in one of two ways: the first might be to have students create background sound effects to the story while it is being read; the second would be to play pre-recorded music that fits the story. A recording of Chinese music, particularly Chinese symphonic music, would be especially appropriate. Once students become familiar with their sound effects or the recording, they can musically accompany classmates who either read the book aloud or tell the story from their visual story maps.

Interpersonal Activity:

The teacher might make a board game with a format similar to *Candy Land* or *Snakes and Ladders*. This game would be something like *Rivers and Falls* or the *Yangtze River Game*; it involves taking a winding river path back to a houseboat. Along the way, numerous penalties or boons are possible.

A large piece of cardstock or butcher paper is needed for the game board. To make the game, tape two blue markers together and draw parallel lines that wind around the entire game board. This is the river. Next divide the river up into one-inch squares to mark the progress of the players along the board. Then add connecting paths between the meanders of the river. These can be waterfalls that students can slide down or bridges to advance upwards. Finally, the game board can be embellished in any way the teacher chooses.

Four to six students can play the game at one time with dice, cards, or a spinner to advance around the board. A round spinner attached to the game board with a brad eliminates the problem of lost pieces.

By adding a deck of cards with problems to solve, the game can easily incorporate thinking skills or problem-solving in addition to pure chance. Cards can be drawn when students land on previously marked squares, perhaps called *Ping* squares.

Sample problems might include:

- Tell the other players how a duck might escape from a mean boy who was try-ing to catch it. Then move forward 3 spaces.
- Name one advantage a duck has over other animals, then move forward one square.
- Tell why water pollution would be a problem for Ping. If the group approves your answer, move to the next bridge.
- Why do you think ducks sleep with their beaks on their backs? Move forward three spaces if you can explain the answer.
- If one player left this game, the way Ping left his brothers and sisters, how would the departure affect the other players? Talk about this with your group, and then move ahead two spaces.

Intrapersonal Activity:

The Story about Ping provides a wonderful opportunity for children to discuss something most of them fear and many have experienced — being lost. The teacher can lead a group discussion that asks

- What is it like to be lost?
- How does it feel?
- What else causes those kinds of feelings?
- What is the best thing to do when you are lost?
- How can you prevent yourself from getting lost?

After a brief discussion, students might be asked to illustrate fear and happiness.

Assessment:

A simple assessment activity is to ask students to tell the story of Ping to an older student, parent, or other adult. The listener can fill out a brief questionnaire that emphasizes whether the student was capable of relaying key points of the story. For example:

- What was Ping?
- Where did Ping live?
- What happened to Ping?
- Did the student add colorful details?
- Did the student tell the story with the proper sequence of events?

LESSON #9:   *ANIMAL FARM* BY GEORGE ORWELL

Subject Area:	Language Arts/Social Studies
Main Concept:	Totalitarianism
Principle To Be Taught:	Things are not always as they appear to be
Unit:	Forms of government or leadership
Previous Lesson:	Examples of democracies
Following Lesson:	Examples of monarchies
Grade Level:	6-12

Materials Needed:	Copies of *Animal Farm* by George Orwell

Linguistic Activity:

Many intermediate and secondary students enjoy George Orwell's *Animal Farm*, an animal fable that satirizes communism. There are several ways that the reading of the story might be approached. I've listed a few below:

1. The teacher reads the story aloud as students follow along in their books.

2. Small groups of students take turns reading the story aloud to each other.

3. The teacher or another adult tape records the story page-by-page onto a cassette tape. At the end of each page, space is left for a student to tape record himself reading the story. This is an effective approach for students who struggle with reading. They can listen to the story and then practice reading the taped portions at their own rate.

4. Students can be assigned portions of the book to read and reflect on in their journals.

After the students have read the story, the teacher may want them to discuss the following questions:

1. Who are the characters?
2. What is the setting?
3. What do the animals want?
4. What specific course of events led to the pigs taking charge of the farm?
5. How were the other animals involved in taking over the farm?
6. How did Napoleon rise to power?
7. Once Napoleon took charge, what control did the other animals actually have over their own lives?
8. Why did the animals continue to believe in Napoleon?
9. What prevented the other animals from challenging Napoleon and his power?
10. Do such events happen in human society? Can you provide any examples?

Logical-Mathematical Activity:

For an exercise examining cause and effect in the book, ask students to make a chart showing how the actions of Napoleon and his supporters led to the downfall of the ideals the animals had envisioned. Under "Causes," list Napoleon's actions. Under "Effects," list the results his actions had. This could lead to a discussion about whether certain actions which appear benevolent necessarily are.

CAUSES	EFFECTS

 Kinesthetic Activity:

Many scenes from *Animal Farm* can be dramatized easily. One scene occurs in the barn when Napoleon first informs the other animals that he is in charge now. This scene could be scripted from the text or simply improvised. Students can be organized into small groups to rehearse their scenes, or the teacher might request volunteers who are willing to improvise the scene just after it has been read.

 Visual-Spatial Activity:

Students create maps of the farm which include the following:
1. the barns
2. the farmer's house
3. the pastures and fields
4. the site of the windmill
5. the neighboring farms
6. the roads
7. the site of the battle

Once the maps are drawn, students should label what events took place where.

Musical Activity:

The pigs in Animal Farm relied upon chants and slogans to implant their ideas into the minds of their fellow animals. Students could be asked to recall musical commercials that attempt to sell their products with catchy phrases. Students can compile lists of musical phrases from current commercials and then create counter-slogans to convince people not to buy such products.

Interpersonal Activity:

Working in groups, students can determine their ideal form of classroom or schoolwide governance. To begin their planning they may want to reflect on the following questions:

- How should leaders be selected?
- What should be the limits of a leader's power?
- What laws are most essential?
- What are the consequences of breaking the laws?
- How can all students effectively participate in their government?
- Could young people be responsible for self-governance? Why or why not?
- At what age could they be responsible for what kinds of self-governance?

Each group should share their form of governance with the class and perhaps decide which components might be implemented in governing the classroom.

Intrapersonal Activity:

In brief essays, students could respond to the following questions:

- Which character did you most relate to in Animal Farm and why?
- What form of government do you prefer and why?
- What role would you want to play in government and why?

Assessment:

Teachers may want to collect the cause and effect charts or the maps the students have made.

LESSON #10:   **HARRIET TUBMAN AND THE**
                                   UNDERGROUND RAILROAD

Subject Area: Social Studies

Main Concept: Personal courage

Principle To Be Taught: Some people find it necessary to take action
                                      against social injustice

Unit: 19th Century American history

Previous Lesson: The life of a slave

Following Lesson: The abolitionists

Grade level: 3-8

Materials Needed: Information on Harriet Tubman and the
                                      Underground Railroad

                                   Maps of the eastern United States

                                   Diorama materials such as large pieces of
                                      cardboard or cardstock, twigs, colored
                                      construction paper, popsicle sticks, etc.

                                   A selection of Negro spirituals as well as one
                                      or more songs from the Civil Rights
                                      Movement of the 1960's

Linguistic Activity:

Teachers should locate information on Harriet Tubman. Several biographies and encyclopedic entries are available, and many basal readers contain stories about her. Teachers can learn about Harriet Tubman's life and accomplishments, and share their findings with students in the form of a story. After the storytelling is completed, a discussion of slavery, freedom, and injustice might follow with the teacher encouraging students to think about the right course of action in an unjust situation.

Logical-Mathematical Activity:

There are numerous story problems that can help students understand Harriet Tubman's accomplishments. Depending upon the grade level of students, the story problems may require addition, subtraction, multiplication, division, or decimals and percentages. Some examples follow:

1. Harriet Tubman made 19 trips on the Underground Railroad. She took about 16 slaves on each trip. How many slaves did she bring to freedom altogether?

2. If Harriet brought 28 slaves to freedom in 1850 and 37 slaves in 1851, how many slaves did she save during those two years?

3. If there were 2,800 slaves in Maryland and Harriet Tubman saved 300 of them, what percentage did she rescue?

4. If Harriet had to hide 42 of her companions under a load of straw on a wagon but only 7 of them would fit in one wagon, how many trips would the wagon have to make to hide all of them?

5. If you were helping Harriet Tubman lead 15 slaves to freedom and you came to a bridge with a guard on either end, how would you get the slaves across the bridge without getting caught?

Kinesthetic Activity:

Working in small groups, students can make dioramas depicting scenes along the Underground Railroad. Before they start working, each group should decide and explain what portion of the Underground Railroad they will create to avoid duplication among the dioramas.

Visual-Spatial Activity:

On a blank map of the eastern United States, students can be asked to identify various points of the Underground Railroad, noting states, cities, towns, and hiding places along the route.

Musical Activity:

There are many old Negro spirituals which the slaves sang on their route to the North. Students could learn one of these songs, either from recordings or by having someone who knows them come in and teach them. Here is a brief list:

> Do, Lord
> Go Tell It On the Mountain
> He's Got the Whole World
> I'm Gonna Do What the Spirit Says
> Jacob's Ladder
> Joshua Fought the Battle of Jericho
> Nobody Knows the Trouble I've Seen
> Old-Time Religion
> Rock-a My Soul
> Steal Away
> Swing Low, Sweet Chariot

In addition, songs like the ones listed below emerged during the American civil rights movement in the 1960's and came from or referred back to the time of Harriet Tubman. In fact, in 1977 Walter Robinson wrote a song entitled "Harriet Tubman."

Amen	Harriet Tubman
I'm On My Way	John Brown's Body
Michael Row	We Shall Overcome
This Little Light	

Students can learn one or more songs from each era, and compare and contrast what the lyrics reveal. All the above songs can be found in *Rise Up Singing* by Peter Blood-Patterson.

Interpersonal Activity:

Harriet Tubman courageously took action against social injustice. Her life can serve as a model for students, inspiring them to become aware of such issues such as homelessness, poverty, lack of medical care, or abuse.

With students, discuss local problems in their community to determine if there is one they would like to tackle. Develop a realistic action plan to address the problem, and start work on your own Harriet Tubman community action service project. Some of the service projects I have done with my students include conducting food drives, visiting retirement homes, cleaning local parks, and collecting pennies for UNICEF.

Intrapersonal Activity:

When considering important social problems, students can clarify the values that are most important to them, such as altruism, compassion, courage, generosity, kindness, helpfulness, or tolerance. In their journals, students can select one value, define it, and reflect on how to express that value in their lives. Student reflections might lead to a bulletin board on values, letters to the editor, or a "class book of values."

Assessment:

To assess students' knowledge about Harriet Tubman and her accomplishments, students might describe her ideals and beliefs and how she implemented them. This could be done in written or visual formats. As an alternative, teachers might suggest that students write song lyrics that include this information. Students can also explain what distinguishes someone like Harriet Tubman from other people who may hold similar beliefs but don't act upon them.

LESSON # 11:   WEATHER

Subject Area:	Science
Main Concept:	Weather affects our lives in many ways
Principle To Be Taught:	Humans react and try to be proactive to weather patterns
Unit:	Earth's atmosphere and climate
Previous Lesson:	Climates
Following Lesson:	Weather in different geographical regions
Grade Level:	3 - 8
Materials Needed:	Copies of newspapers
	Outdoor thermometer
	"Weather" music such as Vivaldi's The *Four Seasons* or Grofé's *Grand Canyon Suite*
	Photocopies of the following visual-spatial, interpersonal, and intrapersonal activities for all students

Linguistic Activity:

Provide students with copies of newspapers. It would be worthwhile to have newspapers from a variety of climates and geographical regions as well as from different times of the year. Suggest that students read articles on weather and its effects. Discuss how weather affects people, and how people have learned to respond to various weather conditions. You may want to list student responses on the board or on a large piece of butcher paper to keep posted in the classroom.

Logical-Mathematical Activity:

Place an outdoor thermometer near a classroom window or other location where students can check it readily. Select different students to record daily and hourly temperatures over an extended period of time. Ask all students to maintain a chart of the weather. On the same chart, they can also track what people wear and do because of the weather. After they have kept the chart for several weeks, they can use it to make generalizations and predictions about the weather.

Kinesthetic Activity:

For younger students, suggest they pantomime how people respond to different types of weather. Using an open space, give verbal cues such as:

- Show with your body how you feel when it is over 100°.
- Show how you feel on a cold, snowy day.
- How do you move on ice?
- How would you move if a hurricane were blowing?
- How would you act after a hurricane had passed?
- Show how would you feel if you heard it was going to rain tomorrow and it was the day for a class picnic or outdoor field trip.
- Show how you would move in a thick fog.
- Show what you would do if you went outside and found two feet of snow on the ground.

After practicing movements for various types of weather, working in small groups, students can create their own pantomimes for the rest of the class. These short skits can depict clothing, movement, activities, and reactions to various types of weather.

For older students, ask that they work in small groups to produce television weather forecasts. Each person should assume a role, such as statistician, illustrator, announcer, script writer, meteorological expert, video-camera person, and producer. Require that students use real data that incorporates the four elements of weather (temperature, air pressure, wind, and moisture) as well as accurate visuals. Also require that they specify how people will respond to the various weather patterns.

Visual-Spatial Activity:

Students can draw individual pictures that illustrate the four main elements of weather: temperature, air pressure, wind, and moisture.

Temperature: the degree of heat in the atmosphere	*Air Pressure: the force of the atmosphere on earth*
Moisture: the water cycle vapor—water—clouds—rain	*Wind: the movemet of air from high presure to low*

Students could also be asked to illustrate other weather phenomena: the water cycle, global wind patterns, movements of air masses as shown on TV weather reports, the formation of warm and cold fronts, how geographical features affect weather, different kinds of storms, or weather maps which show high and low temperatures in different states or countries.

Musical Activity:

Students can listen to Vivaldi's *The Four Seasons* or Ferde Grofé's *The Grand Canyon Suite*, both of which depict different types of weather. Students can listen to entire compositions or pre-selected pieces to determine how the composers created the sounds and moods for various types of weather.

Interpersonal Activity:

Students usually enjoy scavenger hunts and the following activity introduces them to weather vocabulary. Divide students into groups of four to five. Provide each group with a list of weather terms and inform them that they must find the meanings of as many of the words as possible within a 24 hour period. They must also describe the impact of any of these weather phenomena on people. The information can be retrieved by looking the terms up, by asking other people, or by calling the library or local experts at a nearby university. Also tell students that they must devise a plan for working together efficiently before they begin.

Before students begin seeking their definitions, it may be wise to first discuss what constitutes a good definition. Students could be given examples to determine what is an effective definition and what isn't. They can practice making their own definitions and should be directed to paraphrase, not copy, the definitions of weather terms.

SCAVENGER HUNT OF WEATHER TERMS

air	humidity	squall
air pressure	hurricane	storm
barometer	hygrometer	temperature
blizzard	ice	thermometer
chinook	jet stream	thunder
cloud	lightning	tornado
cloudburst	monsoon	trade wind
cold front	northern	typhoon
cyclone	prevailing westerly	vapor
dew	rain	warm front
doldrums	rainbow	waterspout
drought	rain gauge	weather balloon
dust storm	sandstorm	weather vane
fog	sirocco	whirlwind
frost	sleet	wind
hail	snow	

Intrapersonal Activity:

Ask students to reflect on weather with the following questions:

What is your favorite type of weather? Why?_____
_____

What is your least favorite type of weather? Why? _____
_____

If you had to choose between living in a very, very hot place and a very, very cold place, which would you choose? Why? _____
_____

How do rainy days make you feel? Why?_____
_____

How do sunny days make your feel? Why? _____
_____

How do snowy days make you feel? Why? _____
_____

How do storms make you feel? Why? _____
_____

How does wind make you feel? Why? _____
_____

If you compared yourself to one kind of weather, what would it be and why?
_____
_____

If you could be one of the four main components of weather, which would it be and why?
_____

Scientists have developed a large plastic dome that is airtight and contains controlled weather. It has living quarters, gardens, and recreational areas. People have lived in it for up to two years. Would you choose to live in an environment where the weather was completely controlled, or would you prefer to have the uncertainty of normal weather? Why?
_____
_____

Assessment:

Students can be asked to illustrate the meanings of several weather terms from their scavenger hunt.

LESSON # 12:   SPRING

Subject Area:	Language Arts
Main Concept:	Each season has unique characteristics
Principle To Be Taught:	Life is continually changing
Unit:	Seasons and Why They Happen
Previous Lesson:	Winter
Following Lesson:	Summer
Grade level:	3-6

Materials Needed:
Ezra Jack Keats' book, *In a Spring Garden*
Star charts
Seeds and paper cups, or garden supplies
Raisins and toothpicks
Photocopies of musical and intrapersonal activities

Linguistic Activity:

Following a walk outside to observe signs of spring, students can read Ezra Jack Keats' book *In A Spring Garden* and other poems about spring. Provide students with an opening line from a poem about spring and ask that they create subsequent lines. Each student should write at least one or more poems about spring. Once written and read to the class, gather all of the student-written poems and bind them into a class book with at least one poem by each student. Create a title such as *Reflections on Spring* or *In A Spring Classroom*.

Logical-Mathematical Activity:

Several quantitative activities can focus on spring. Students can be asked to count the hours and minutes of daylight. The data can be gathered from an almanac or the daily paper which provides exact times. Students can calculate how much longer each day is than previous ones and keep track for several days or weeks.

Students can also measure the growth of new shoots, branches, or plants, or grow beans, pumpkins, or sunflowers in cups, and measure their daily growth. Even grass can be measured on a daily basis.

Another possibility is for students to contrast spring in The Northern and Southern Hemispheres, or spring at the North and South Poles.

Students might research and explain how the seasons change on earth. Some may want to make small models to replicate this phenomenon.

Kinesthetic Activity:

Classrooms can turn into beautiful spring gardens! Try growing mung bean sprouts for snacks, or any other kind of garden vegetables or flowers from seeds in paper cups. (One packet will be enough for the whole class.) Also sweet potatoes, carrots, parsnips, or other root vegetables can be turned into attractive plants; students can simply cut off the roots about an inch below the top and place them in dishes of water. The plants will grow new shoots in a few days. Also avocado pits grow into tiny trees when half-submerged in water. Place the pointed end up.

If the school has outdoor garden space, inquire whether someone can rototil a patch of soil for a garden. If this is possible, involve students in planning the garden by creating a budget, planning the crops, making the garden, and distributing the results. The students in one school in south-central Los Angeles actually turned their garden into a profitable business creating a fund for college scholarships for those going on to higher education.

Visual-Spatial Activity:

Provide students with star charts of the constellations, identifying those that appear in the spring sky. Have students select one or two constellations to make with raisins and toothpicks. Students may also research facts about the constellations they make.

Musical Activity:

Share William Blake's poem entitled "Spring" with students.

Sound the Flute!
Now it's mute.
Birds delight
Day and Night;
Nightingale
In the dale,
Lake in Sky,
Merrily,
Merrily, Merrily to welcome in the Year.

Little Boy
Full of joy;
Little girl,
Sweet and small;
Cock does crow,
So do you;
Merry voice,
Infant noise,
Merrily, Merrily to welcome in the Year.

Little Lamb,
Here I am;
Come and lick
My white neck;
Let me pull
Your soft Wool'
Let me kiss
Your soft face:
Merrily, Merrily, we welcome in the Year.

Change the refrain to "Merrily, Merrily, we welcome in the spring." Then suggest that students write their own single-phrase descriptors of spring. String the phrases together in verses of five or six lines with the new refrain inserted at the end of each verse.

The class will now have a spring song for choral reading. Each student can read his or her lines as they appear in the newly composed song. At the end of each verse, the entire class recites the refrain. It will sound rhythmical and can be further enhanced by creating a melody for the refrain. The song can be adapted for other seasons as well.

Interpersonal Activity:

Organize students into groups. Each group chooses one country or geographical region to study. Using encyclopedias, social studies texts, interviews with individuals from diverse cultures, or other resources, each group studies how spring is celebrated in another culture or region. Although many modern cultures do not celebrate spring itself, most have some form of religious, traditional, or even political festival during the spring. Easter, May Day, and ancient Celtic equinox celebrations are examples of springtime rites. When their research is complete, the groups might present what they learned to the rest of the class.

Intrapersonal Activity:

Discuss the changes that each season brings with students. Ask them to compare such changes in nature to changes within themselves. The discussion might focus on the following question: Seasons change, how have you changed, and how will you change in the future? Students can then write poetic responses to the following:

Before I was _____

Now I am _____

Next I will be _____

Before I was _____

Now I am _____

Next I will be _____

Before I was _____

Now I am _____

Next I will be _____

And the way I will always remain the same is _____

_____

Assessment:

Make a collage of pictures and words about spring. The pictures can be drawn or cut from old magazines or seed catalogs. The collage should depict at least ten characteristics of spring, such as flowers blooming, frogs croaking, birds being born, days getting longer, spring constellations visible in The Northern Hemisphere, and the occurrence of holidays or festivals around the world.

LESSON #13:   CIRCUMFERENCE AND DIAMETER

Subject Area:	Math
Main Concept:	Relationships within geometric shapes
Principle To Be Taught:	Pi is the relationship between the circumference and the diameter of a circle.
Unit:	Measurement
Previous Lesson:	Calculating circumference and area of circles
Following Lesson:	Finding and measuring real circles
Grade level:	5-12
Materials Needed:	Information about circumference and diameter
	Photocopies of the math problems from the logical-mathematical activity, the song from the musical activity, and the quote from the intrapersonal activity for each student
	Large pieces of twine for each pair of students
	Protractors, rulers, compasses, circle templates, scissors, colored paper
	Simple musical instruments
	One eight or ten inch paper circle for each student

Linguistic Activity:

To introduce students to the concept of Pi, the teacher can make a presentation about the relationship between circumference and diameter or ask students to read a fact sheet which contains such information. The fact sheet can be taken from a text book or an encyclopedia entry under "Circles." After students have read the information, they might be asked to write a three-line verse about circles, diameters, and circumference.

Logical-Mathematical Activity:

Using the formulas for determining diameter and circumference, students can solve problems such as the following. This sheet has been written to photocopy to give to students.

Circumference = π d	Area = π r^2

The radius of a circle is 5 centimeters (cm).
    a. What is the circumference of the circle? _____
    b. What is the area of the circle?   _____

The radius of a circle is 12 cm.
    a. What is the circumference of the circle? _____
    b. What is the area of the circle?   _____

The diameter of a circle is 43 meters (m).
    a. What is the circumference of the circle? _____
    b. What is the area of the circle?   _____

The diameter of a circle is 15 miles.
    a. What is the circumference of the circle? _____
    b. What is the area of the circle?   _____

The area of a circle is 452.16 square centimeters.
    a. What is the radius of the circle?   _____
    b. What is the circumference of the circle? _____

When you have finished these problems, you can make up problems of your own using the above formulas.

Kinesthetic Activity:

Remind students of the rule:

The circumference of a circle is always just a little more than three diameters, no matter what the size of the circle.

Have students work in pairs or small groups. One student at a time forms a circle with his or her arms. Another student who has a piece of twine should measure the diameter and circumference of his classmate's circle, determining the relationship of the two to each other. Students should try at least three different sizes of circles to confirm that the relationship is consistent.

To extend the activity, students might invent another way to demonstrate this relationship kinesthetically.

Visual-Spatial Activity:

Using compasses, protractors, circle templates, colored paper, scissors, and rulers, students can create artistic compositions that include only circles and straight lines. Students should be told that the circles can be any size but the straight lines must be the same length as the circumferences, diameters, or radii of the circles (or about 3.14 times the diameter).

Musical Activity:

Provide students with some simple instruments and have them create musical accompaniment for the song below.

A Circular Song

We use circles every day.
They help us ride our bikes away.
We see circles through a round eye.
And we know 3.14 is Pi.

Diameters cut circles in two.
To get circumference, here's what you do:
Multiply the diameter by 3.14.
Now wasn't that an easy chore?

An additional musical activity which would allow students to experience circularity would be singing in rounds. A list of rounds is included here. With three groups singing parts to a round several times through, students should begin to see how even music can move in circles.

Rounds

O How Lovely is the Evening
One Bottle of Pop
Scotland's Burning
Kookaburra
Make New Friends
Hey Ho, Nobody Home
I Love the Flowers
Come Follow
Row, Row
Jubilate

Interpersonal Activity:

Students work in pairs. Each student is provided with a paper circle 8" to 10" in diameter. One person is the reader; the other is the folder. The folder takes a paper circle. The reader reads the following directions as the folder follows them.

Fold the circle in half and crease along the diameter.

Fold the circle in half again, forming two perpendicular radii.

Unfold the paper.

Using the endpoints of two adjacent diameter lines, fold in the flap connecting them, thus forming a side.

Repeat the same action with the three remaining sides.

What shape do you have?

What is the relationship of the length of each side to the circle?

Next the partners switch roles. After completing this exercise, students can work together to see how many other shapes they can make with the original circle. Can they make triangles, octagons, trapezoids?

Intrapersonal Activity:

Provide students with copies of the following:

Excerpt from Ralph Waldo Emerson's essay "Circles."

The life of a man is a self-evolving circle, which, from a ring imperceptibly small, rushes on all sides outwards to new and larger circles, and that without end. The extent to which this generation of circles, wheel without wheel, will go, depends on the force or truth of the individual soul. For it is the inert effort of each thought, having formed itself into a circular way of circumstance, . . . to heap itself on that ridge, and to solidify, and hem in the life. But if the soul is quick and strong, it bursts over that boundary on all sides, and expands another orbit on the great deep, which also runs up into a high wave, with attempt again to stop and to bind. But the heart refuses to be imprisoned; in its first and narrowest pulse it already tends outward with a vast force, and to immense and innumerable expansions.

When they are finished, students can reflect upon what they have read, using the following questions and discussing their thoughts with someone else.

1. How are our lives circular?
2. How do we move from one circle in our lives to the next?
3. Do our circles overlap with each other's?
4. Are there family circles, group circles, national circles, circles of civilization or human evolution?

If the passage is too difficult for students, the concept of one's life metaphorically expanding outward like a circle can be presented by the teacher and discussed with the class.

Assessment:

Students can demonstrate their understanding of Pi by solving problems in the logical-mathematical or kinesthetic activities provided above.

LESSON #14:   COMETS

Subject Area:	Science/Astronomy
Main Concept:	Comets are objects that orbit the sun
Principle To Be Taught:	The universe is filled with fascinating objects
Unit:	The Solar System
Previous Lesson:	Planets
Following Lesson:	Asteroids
Grade level:	4-9
Materials Needed:	Photocopies of the linguistic, musical, mathematical, intrapersonal, and assessment activities below
	Marshmallows (if they are unavailable, crumpled pieces of paper will suffice)
	Soda straws or short sticks (even toothpicks could work)
	Curling ribbon, yarn, or string
	Science books
	Graph paper with small squares
	Cardstock
	Rulers
	Scissors
	Blue construction paper
	White glue in squeeze bottles, and gold, silver, multi-colored glitter or other art materials
	Percussion instruments from the music room or homemade ones

 Linguistic Activity:

Teachers can provide a brief lecture on comets and/or ask students to read information from their science books or the fact sheet provided on the next page:

Comet Fact Sheet

Comets look like fuzzy stars with tails. They consist of balls of ice, gas, and dust. Comets travel through the solar system along egg-shaped orbits called ellipses. All comets circle the sun because they are locked into the sun's gravity field in the same way planets which circle the sun are locked into its gravity field. Some comets have short orbits and can circle the sun in a matter of months. Others have elongated orbits requiring several hundred years to circle the sun.

The long, shiny tails of comets develop as they draw near to the sun and some tails may stretch over 100 million miles in length. As a comet approaches the sun, the heat causes the icy nucleus to evaporate and to form a coma around the nucleus. The pressure of the sun's light then pushes the small particles of dust away from the coma forming the tail. All a comet's light comes indirectly from the sun. What is visible to people is the reflection of sunlight off the coma and tail of a comet.

The tail of a comet always points away from the sun, causing the tail to trail behind the comet as it approaches the sun. However, after circling the sun and beginning the outward journey in its elongated orbit, the tail actually leads the nucleus of the comet.

One of the most famous comets is Halley's Comet which appears about every 77 years. It was last seen in 1986 and was visible as it crossed through earth's orbit.

When students have read the fact sheet, they can respond in writing to the following questions:

1. What word describes the shape of a comet's orbit? [ellipse, cigar, etc.]
2. What is the center of the ball of a comet called? [nucleus]
3. What is the name of the hazy cloud surrounding the center of the ball? [coma]
4. What causes a comet to have a tail? [pressure of the sun's light]
5. Name at least one famous comet. [Halley's, Kohoutek, Bennett,...]
6. When does the tail of a comet lead? [as it travels away from the sun]
7. What are comets made of? [ice, gas, dust]
8. How are comets similar to planets? [they orbit the sun]
9. How are comets different from planets?
   [their orbits are more elongated, they have tails]
10. Why do you think comets have such strange orbits?
    [answers may vary; e.g. perhaps because they form at the furthest edge of the solar system]

Logical-Mathematical Activity:

Provide students with graph paper. Tell them that their task is to calculate and draw the tails of different-sized comets on graph paper. Some sample problems follow:

COMET MATH

1. Draw a small comet. Then draw a tail which is 5 cm. long.

2. Draw a comet. Then draw a tail which is 15 cm. long.

3. Draw a comet. Then draw a tail which is 25 cm. long.

4. Draw a comet. Then draw a tail which is 2 in. long.

5. Draw a comet. Then draw a tail which is 5 in. long.

6. Draw a comet to fill one square of the graph paper.
   Draw a tail 5 times the length of the comet.

7. Draw a comet to fill one square of the graph paper.
   Draw a tail 10 times the length of the comet.

8. Draw a comet to fill one square of the graph paper.
   Draw a tail 22 times the length of the comet.

9. Draw a comet to fill one square of the graph paper.
   Then find a way to draw a tail 50 times the length of the comet.

10. Draw a comet to fill one square of the graph paper.
    Then find a way to draw a tail 100 times the length of the comet.

 Kinesthetic Activity:

Suggest that students construct their own comets from marshmallows, drinking straws or small sticks, ribbon, or string (see sample). Then carrying their hand-made comets, they can simulate the orbit of a real comet by walking around "the sun" while pointing their comet tails away from it.

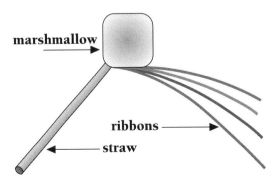

marshmallow

ribbons

straw

Visual-Spatial Activity:

Students can create comet art. Explain that students will create a visual of a comet with the nucleus, coma, and tail properly labeled. Provide them with construction paper and art supplies. Suggest that the comet art can be drawn, painted, made with glue and glitter, colored sticky-dots and yarn, or other

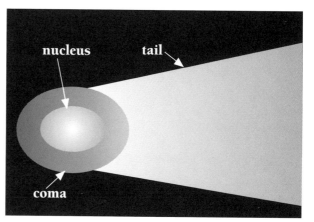

art materials. The sample above could easily be made with white glue and glitter.

Musical Activity:

Students can create stanzas to add to the following song. The melody for this song is Twinkle, Twinkle Little Star. In small groups, students should write additional stanzas of six lines. Each group can teach the rest of the class their additional lyrics.

Students can also accompany the song with percussion instruments from the music room or homemade ones such as sandpaper, jars with beans for shakers, rhythm sticks, and large nails. To keep the noise level down soft percussion instruments such as bean-bags, styrofoam, small sticks, and shakers with raisins or small marshmallows inside should be used.

A Comet Song
(to the tune of *Twinkle, Twinkle...*)

Comet, comet, up so high,
A fuzzy streak across the sky.
A ball of ice and dust and gas,
A tail behind you as you pass.
Comet, comet, as you burn,
We will wait for your return.

Comet, comet, up so high,
Streaking back across the sky.
A ball of ice and dust and gas,
Your tail before you as you pass.
Comet, comet, far away,
Please come back again some day.

Interpersonal Activity:

Organize students into small groups. Each group will make one fact puzzle about comets. A fact puzzle requires a sheet of cardstock (or construction paper), 8" X 11" or larger. Each person in the group should make at least one piece of the puzzle. Students begin by writing "comets" in the center of the cardstock. They then draw wavy lines to the edges of the paper to define the pieces. Before cutting out any puzzle piece, students should color the back side of the puzzle to distinguish front from back visually. Next they cut out their pieces with each student writing a fact on his or her piece. One-at-a-time, students take turns putting together their puzzle and others from different groups. As students fit the puzzles together, ask them to take time to learn and reflect on the information the puzzle contains. (See sample below.)

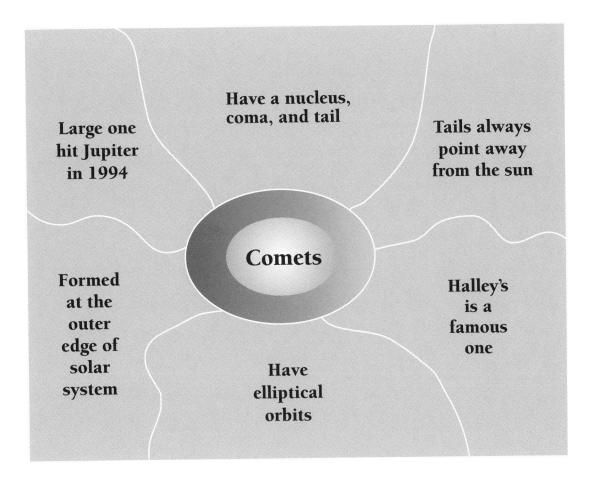

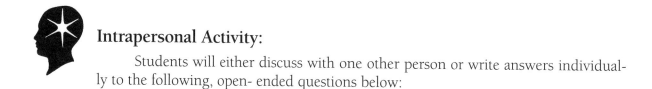

Intrapersonal Activity:

Students will either discuss with one other person or write answers individually to the following, open- ended questions below:

Name _____

Comet Questions for Consideration

1. If you were to take a long journey into space to explore distant comets, list ten things you would want to take with you.

2. If you were to be gone for ten years on this journey, what feelings do you think you would have before leaving?

3. With whom would you share your feelings and how would you share them?

4. In what ways do you think you might change during the time you are gone?

5. The orbit of a comet is cyclical; that is, it returns at regular intervals. What are some things in your life that happen at regular intervals such as daily, weekly, monthly, yearly or longer?

6. Do you like things in your life to happen at regular intervals or do you prefer unexpected spontaneous things to happen? Why?

Assessment:

To evaluate student learning about comets, provide students with assessment options. Give them the following list and let them choose the option that is of most interest to them.

Choices for Assessment:

Write a 1-to-2 page report about comets. Use at least three sources of information. Include a title page, a bibliography, and at least one diagram. The report should be typed or written neatly.

Write a song about comets which includes at least five facts and some type of musical accompaniment. Either use a melody you already know or create your own.

Conduct a mock interview about comets with an "expert". One person could be the interviewer, the other a scientist. Include 5 to 10 important facts about comets in your interview.

Create a diagram or poster about comets. The poster should include information about the physical structure of comets, their orbits, and how they appear to humans on earth.

Choose any one of the items above and work on it collaboratively with a friend. If this choice is made, both students should take responsibility for certain parts of the work.

Choose your own method of presenting what you have learned about comets. Please obtain approval from your teacher prior to beginning your project.

Take a written test. The questions provided for the linguistic activity above could be used as test items.

LESSON # 15:   THE BOSTON TEA PARTY

Subject Area:	Social Studies
Main Concept:	Independence
Principle To Be Taught:	"Might" doesn't always make "right"
Unit:	Causes of the American Revolution
Previous Lesson:	British acts imposed on the colonists
Following Lesson:	The start of the Revolutionary War
Grade level:	3-10
Materials needed:	Copies of Patrick Henry's "Give me liberty or give me death" speech
	Butcher paper, cash register tape, or sheets of 9 X 18 construction paper taped together for student timelines
	Photocopies of visual, interpersonal, intrapersonal, and musical activities

Linguistic Activity:

The Boston Tea Party was a turning point in British-colonial relations, and is a subject studied in many classrooms. After students have learned the causes of the revolt, they might read Patrick Henry's "Give me liberty or give me death" speech given in 1775. Students can similarly compose "a call to arms" speech to inspire their fellow citizens to rise up against the British.

The speech must include several good reasons for revolt such as the Stamp Act or the Sugar Act. It also must include at least three good reasons why the populace should rebel. The speech should be at least three minutes long, have a greeting at the beginning such as, "My fellow citizens," and a strong conclusion, such as "For these reasons, I urge you to follow me now as we take up arms against the British. Rise up my friends. Rebel!"

To present other perspectives, alternative speeches could be made such as a "call to peace" by the pacifists, a call for resolution of the conflict" by mediators, a "call to leave the country" by the Native Americans, or a "call to subdue" by the British. In each case, the speech must present good reasons why the audience should follow the advice of the speaker. These reasons should be based upon actual circumstances preceding the Boston Tea Party.

As an extension activity, students could be encouraged to make similar speeches (or written narratives) about topics of interest to them. For example, they might make a plea to have no homework for a week or a plea for sixth graders to tutor younger students at the school.

Logical-Mathematical Activity:

Students can create a timeline of events leading up to the Boston Tea Party. The timeline might be done in vertical form on lined paper, in book form with each page highlighting a different event, in a calendar format, or simply on a "line" as shown below.

This example of a timeline shows only a few of the many events that led up to the American Revolution.

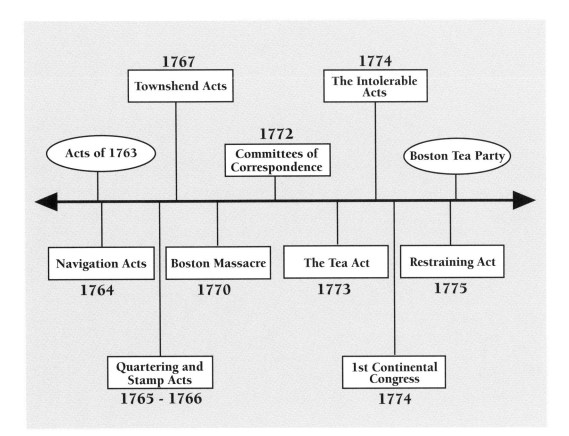

Kinesthetic Activity:

The following is a narrative pantomime of the Boston Tea Party to be read aloud by the teacher while the students silently pantomime the scene. The only rule is that students can not touch anyone else during the pantomime. Practice reading through the narrative ahead of time and when reading to the class, monitor student reactions and pause or move ahead as appropriate. Emphasize opportunities for students to use their imaginations to see, smell, hear, and touch the events. It is the senses which will bring the experience to life.

[Reader: Explain to students they will do a few warm-ups before starting the pantomime of the Boston Tea Party. Emphasize the underlined words. Pause for…]

Warm-up with students pantomiming the movements:

"How would you creep down a narrow street in the dark if you didn't want anyone to see or hear you?"…"How would you climb up a narrow gangplank onto a ship 30 feet above the water?"…"How would you dump a heavy box over the side of a ship without making any noise?"…

Narrative of the Boston Tea Party for students to pantomime:

You are a young citizen of Boston in 1773. Tonight you are planning a great adventure. To get ready, you have just taken a nap. You are still lying on your bed when you hear the bell on the church steeple ring. You <u>listen carefully</u>… 12 times it rings… midnight. You hear a tapping outside your room… Quickly, but very quietly, you sit up and pull on your boots. Your hands practically shake with excitement as you lace and tie them…

You stand up and pull on your warm coat as you head for the window. Very carefully, you push the shutters open… and climb out… softly touching the ground. Your best friend is waiting for you. With a quick wave to each other you begin sneaking down the dark street together… Cautiously, you peek around the corner… You see other citizens who were at this afternoon's meeting also sneaking down the street toward the waterfront. You wave quietly to them… and then move back into the shadows.

You creep along the street until you come to a door with a feather hanging on it. You signal to your friend that this is where you are all to meet. You tap three times… The door opens and you slip inside… Other citizens like yourself are painting their faces and changing their clothes to look like Indians. You take off your coat and slip into a leather shirt… Then you sit down, take off your boots and put on a pair of leather moccasins… You tie a feather into your hair.

By now, everyone is lined up silently at the door. You creep out and begin sneaking down to the wharf. You pass hand signals back and forth to your friends to let them know the coast is clear... As you draw closer, you can now smell the salt water of Boston Harbor... You can hear the ships creaking in their berths on the pier...You see the ship loaded with tea and you crouch down, hiding in the shadows, waiting for the signal to board...

The signal comes and ever so quietly, watching your balance, you creep up the narrow gangplank onto the boat... Once on board, you quickly find the large crates filled with tea... You wave to your friends to join you... As silently as possible, you open the crates,... smelling the strong smell of tea as they open... You pick up the box and dump the loose tea into the harbor... You work hard for several minutes emptying every box...

At last you are done and the signal goes around to retreat... Watching your balance, you creep back down the gangplank... Back on the pier you turn and watch all of the tea floating on the bay... High fives go around among you and your friends... Then you return home down the same quiet streets... You climb back in your window... turn and wave good night to your best friend... then quietly close the shutters...

You pull the feather from your head and then lie down in bed...and think back through the last few hours... What a great adventure!... Tomorrow at sunrise, you will return to the hall to get your boots and talk with your friends, but now as the church tower strikes two, you slowly drift off to sleep.

Visual-Spatial Activity:

Either before or after the narrative pantomime above, a visual assignment might include drawing a map of the route the colonists took in the pantomime from home to the wharf for the "tea party." The map through Boston could have street names and be turned into a spatial relations activity as students give each other directions to follow on their maps. For example: "if you start at the corner of Lexington and A streets and travel two blocks south and one block west, where would you end up?"

Students could be responsible for drawing their maps, writing their questions, and then checking each other's for correct answers to the questions. This could be done in small groups or pairs. A small scale example follows:

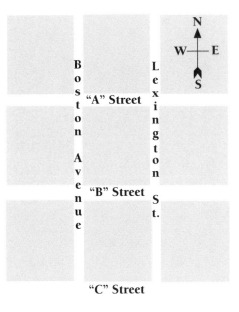

Musical Activity:

The following song is to be sung to the tune of Yankee Doodle and is an easy one for most students to sing since the majority of them already know the melody. Rhythm sticks, tambourines, and triangles provide good accompaniment. Provide students with copies of the song or place a copy on an overhead transparency:

The Boston Tea Party
(Sung to the tune of Yankee Doodle)

*The War of Independence changed
the course of history.
Instead of kings, now people ruled
with democracy.*

*The colonies revolted and fought
England in the war.
They persevered and formed a nation,
free forevermore.*

*It started off one night in Boston,
Men crept on a boat.
They dumped the tea into the bay
And then they watched it float.*

*The colonies revolted and fought
England in the war.
They persevered and formed a nation,
free forevermore.*

*Dressed as Indians, no one knew them
hidden in disguise.
They crept back home triumphantly
with freedom in their eyes.*

*The colonies revolted and fought
England in the war.
They persevered and formed a nation,
free forevermore.*

Interpersonal Activity:

As an interpersonal activity, organize students into groups of 4 to 5 and hand each group the card below or similar ones the teacher has made.

Student directions: In small groups, read the card and follow its directions.

Your group is in charge of planning the Boston Tea Party. Unlike the original planners, you must figure out a way of removing the tea from the ship so it is not wasted. Here are some of the challenges you will face:

1. There are British guards around so you must be quiet.
2. The gangplank will hold only the weight of one man at a time. It will collapse if he is carrying a load.
3. The tea is in boxes that weigh 200 pounds each.
4. The sides of the boat are 20 feet above the dock.

You will need roles for each member of the group. One person is the <u>recorder.</u> The recorder's job is to write down the approach you decide upon. Your strategy must be written, signed by all of you, and turned in. A second person is the <u>illustrator.</u> This person has to draw a picture or diagram of how you will remove the tea. This document will also be turned in. A third person is the <u>facilitator.</u> This person makes certain that the group sticks to the task at hand and involves everyone in the planning. A fourth person is the <u>speaker.</u> This person will present your idea to the whole class without notes. A fifth person can be the <u>timekeeper</u> who is responsible for watching the clock to make sure the group's work is completed in 30 minutes.

Give students the directions and a time limit. To determine roles, ask students to count off within their groups and then announce that all ones will be recorders, all twos will be illustrators, and so on. Or you can have each group select their own roles. If 30 minutes is insufficient, give them extra time. For groups finishing early, they can help their speaker practice, color their illustration, or type out their written description on the class computer.

Intrapersonal Activity:

Some colonists probably felt confusion over rebelling against the British. Many of them had come from England and the British had governed most of the colonies for over 100 years. Suddenly, the colonists were confronted with a choice between loyalty to their king and homeland or freedom and independence. Here is a list of some of the values colonists may have held:

loyalty	determination
friendliness	freedom
trust	tolerance
courage	justice
patience	faithfulness
kindness	dignity
forgiveness	integrity
peace	responsibility

Undoubtedly, many colonists were uncertain about whether to choose loyalty to England or to pursue freedom. Ask students to imagine themselves as colonists and to make a brief presentation about whether they would choose to rebel when they had friends and even family who remained loyal to England.

Assessment:

Use the students' timelines to assess their understanding of events leading up to the Boston Tea Party.

LESSON # 16:

THE SEARCH FOR DELICIOUS BY NATALIE BABBIT

Subject Area:	Language Arts
Main Concept:	Resolving conflict
Principle To Be Taught:	People often incorrectly assume that their way is the only way
Unit:	Fiction
Previous Lesson:	Island of the Blue Dolphins
Following Lesson:	Julie and the Wolves
Grade level:	3-6
Materials Needed:	One or more copies of the book
	Costume box of old clothes, capes, scarves, burlap bags, etc.
	Large boxes for background sets
	Chart from the book for visual activity
	Photocopies of mathematical, interpersonal activities
	12-24 inch boards
	Screw-eyes
	Fishline, wire, or old guitar strings

Linguistic Activity:

Natalie Babbit's book, *The Search for Delicious*, is a wonderful book for intermediate-aged children. It portrays the fictional adventure of a young boy, Vaungaylen, and his journey through his kingdom to determine what people consider to be the most delicious food of all. He encounters a number of intriguing characters and situations along the way. The story revolves around interpersonal conflict and how to manage it.

As a linguistic activity, the students could read the book if a class set is available. If not, the teacher could read the book aloud. For low-ability readers or non-readers, the book could be taped, or others in the class might tutor the non-readers through the book.

As an additional linguistic activity, students might write a character sketch of one of the interesting individuals in the book. Here is a list of characters to choose from:

The Prime Minister	The King	The Queen Gaylen
Hemlock	The General	The Mayor
The Woldweller	Mrs. Copse	Ardis
Pitshaft	Medley	The Minstrel

Student directions might include:

Write a 1-to-2 page description of one of the characters listed on the chalkboard. Tell who they are, where they live, when they enter the story, why they are important in the story, and why you selected that particular character to write about.

Logical-Mathematical Activity:

I have listed several logical possibilities for teachers to choose among:

1. Percentages — students might do a survey to calculate percentages of students who consider Milky Ways, Snickers, or Almond Joys to be the most delicious candy bars.

2. Graphing — students could work with the same statistics as the last activity to create bar graphs, line graphs, or pie charts . There are easy-to-use software applications available for this kind of graphing.

3. Measuring — students might figure distances on Gaylen's journey from scene to scene. Some sample problems are provided below.

4. Story problems — see next page:

Math Problems for *The Search for Delicious*

1. If Gaylen traveled 27 miles from the castle to the first town, 18 miles from the town to the forest, 11 miles further to the apple orchard, 29 miles to the Mildews farm, and then back to the apple orchard, how far did he travel?

   _____

2. If Gaylen left the dwarf's cave at 1:00 PM, traveled for three and one half hours, stopped for lunch for 45 minutes, and traveled again for two hours and twenty minutes to the third town, what time was it when he arrived?

   _____

3. If Gaylen traveled back and forth between the lake and the Nest of the Wind 15 times and the distance between them was 24 miles, then how far did he travel altogether?

   _____

4. If the entire journey from the castle to the lake was 114 miles, but could be cut short 47 miles by going straight from Mrs. Copse's house to the lake, how far would it be taking the shortcut?

   _____

5. If Gaylen traveled 114 miles from the castle to the lake heading east, and the Prime Minister traveled 66 miles from the castle to the lake heading west, how far was a complete trip around the kingdom?

   _____

6. If Hemlock left the castle on Thursday, April 7 and Gaylen left on Saturday, April 9, and Hemlock arrived at the second village on Tuesday, April 19, but it took Gaylen 5 days longer, when did Gaylen get there?

   _____

7. If Gaylen decided to stay with Mrs. Copse, who lived 76 miles from the castle, and if he wanted to visit the Prime Minister four times a year, how far would he travel back and forth in three years?

   _____

Kinesthetic Activity:

The book lends itself naturally to a staged production. There are numerous characters, enough for each person in a class, to portray. There are about five main scenes: the castle, the towns, the forest, the cave, and the lake. Costumes might be minimal or imaginative and ornate.

A script can be written by the teacher, the class as a whole, or small groups working on different scenes. One excellent technique for developing a script is to have students role play different scenes in the play, allowing the script to emerge out of their impromptu dialogues.

If a major production is not practical, small group performances of individual scenes can be great fun. Working in groups of four to six, students can easily portray most of the book's major events. Here are some suggestions:

- The first argument among the king, queen, Hemlock, etc.
- The Mayor, Medley, and Gaylen in the first town
- The woldweller scene (There could be several woldwellers.)
- The scene in the apple orchard (Muzzle and Marrow included.)
- The Mildew's farm
- The Dwarf's cave
- Ardis and Gaylen at the lake
- Hemlock's scene at the lake
- The final scene at the lake (Paper grocery bags stuffed with newspapers make great "rocks" to stack up for a dam.)

Visual-Spatial Activity:

If students plan to dramatize scenes from the book, drawing and painting sets will provide challenging visual activities. Another visual-spatial option is for students to make large picture-story charts of the kingdom, including Gaylen's itinerary. The book contains an illustrated map which can be used as a model.

Musical Activity:

On page 59 of the book, the minstrel sang a song to Gaylen while playing the harp. As a musical activity, students can make their own stringed instruments. Simple materials are required: a piece of wood, screw-eyes, and fishline, wire, or old guitar strings. A cigar box or similar-sized container can add a nice resonating chamber.

To make the stringed instruments, screw two screw-eyes halfway into opposite ends of the stick or board. Tie a piece of wire as tightly as possible to each screw-eye.

Twist the screw-eyes in tightly to tune the string. Using strings of different lengths, creates variation in tones, but the best control of the tone is done by tightening the wires. Any type of tub, bucket, or box underneath the strings will help the sound resonate. The instrument can be used to accompany the minstrel's song or student-made songs.

In addition, students who are learning to play real stringed instruments could bring theirs to class and explain the stringing system as well as how to make different sounds.

Interpersonal Activity:

The book involves numerous examples of interpersonal conflict. Identifying the story's conflicts provides students with opportunities to reflect on and learn ways to resolve or manage conflict. The castle scene, the town scenes, the farm scenes, even the scene at the lake could all have been handled differently if the characters had been willing to negotiate and create win-win outcomes.

A model for conflict negotiation is provided below. Some classes, however, like to develop their own strategies, create a written set of procedures, and practice them with classroom conflicts.

Conflict Resolution

While there are many approaches to resolving conflict,
most involve the following components:

1. Define exactly what the problem is. It is important to avoid using blaming "you" statements, and instead use "I" statements when defining the problem.
2. Brainstorm a list of possible solutions.
3. Choose the best option.
4. Develop an action plan.
5. Implement the action plan.
6. Reflect on whether or not the solution worked and make revisions as needed.

When students are initially learning conflict resolution procedures, it is effective to suggest they work in small rather than large groups. After the students are organized in small groups, identify the steps of conflict resolution and post a chart of the six steps to which they can later refer. Suggest several conflict simulations and ask students to practice resolving each. Once students gain familiarity with the process, ask them to address actual classroom problems.

Intrapersonal Activity:

This story provides an interesting metaphor for students' personal "journeys," in the form of trips they have taken, personal adventures they have had, or their own journeys of growing up. Students can be asked to write about such journeys either in the form of a narrative about one's life, a single, but important incident, or a fictional account of a personal search in which the student is the main character. The journeys might be described in a pattern similar to that of the book. It is important that the teacher or the teacher and students determine the length of the written work, when it is due, and what writing standards are expected.

Assessment:

Just as the Prime Minister created dictionaries in the book, students can create individual dictionaries for assessment. One word (or more) for each letter of the alphabet would provide the book's organization. The class might want to choose a general theme for all student dictionaries such as ways to resolve conflict or thoughts about the story itself, or students might choose individual options.

Multiple Intelligence Lesson Planning Form

For teachers who want to create their own multiple intelligence lessons, a sample format is provided below. This can be photocopied any number of times. Some teachers have enlarged the form to make it easier to capture their ideas. Others have made multiple copies and bound them together to make a lesson plan book.

Lesson Title: _____

Student Outcomes: _____

Activities:

    Linguistic: _____

    _____

    Visual-Spatial: _____

    _____

    Musical: _____

    _____

    Logical-Mathematical:_____

    _____

    Kinesthetic: _____

    _____

    Interpersonal: _____

    _____

    Intrapersonal: _____

    _____

    Assessment:_____

    _____

    _____

Materials & resources needed: _____

_____

Sequence of activities: _____

_____

PART VI: PREPARING FOR SELF-DIRECTED LEARNING

One of the greatest rewards of my Multiple Intelligences teaching has been observing students work in their areas of strength through their independent projects. Many teachers face a dilemma when attempting to integrate Gardner's theory into their classrooms. They wonder whether to emphasize teaching through the seven intelligences on a daily basis or whether to nurture individual student strengths. I choose to do both.

Afternoons in my classroom are primarily dedicated to student projects. For some of their projects, students pursue curriculum topics in greater depth. For others, they study whatever interests them the most. The choices that students make frequently reveal their inherent intelligence strengths. Through the projects students also learn how to plan, manage, and bring closure to their self-selected tasks. So often school missions emphasize creating autonomous learners. I feel fortunate to have found concrete ways to nurture self-directed learning in my students. Some of those strategies follow:

Part VI Contents:

How to Organize Independent Projects

Warming-up to Self-Directed Learning

Eight Steps for Doing Projects

Project Contract

Project Evaluation Form

MI Homework

How to Organize Independent Projects

When I began teaching through the Multiple Intelligences in the mid-1980's, I thought the highlight of my program was the seven learning centers. On a daily basis, students approached content and skills in seven ways. Over the years, however, I have found that the independent project work is the most valuable feature of my program. The projects enable students to apply and further develop the concepts and skills they have gained at the centers. While students enjoy their active, center-based learning, they even more eagerly pursue their independent projects. It is the projects which teach my students how to direct their own learning.

To organize independent projects, students identify their topics, research them for several weeks, plan, and give demonstrations of what they have learned. At the end of each month, I dedicate a few afternoons to student presentations. These are not presentations where students read or give a memorized talk. Instead, they share their learning through skits, songs, poems, stories, dances, interviews, "game shows," charts, posters, diagrams, graphs, puzzles, problems to solve, videotapes, and interactive group activities.

The presentations are informative and engaging. More importantly, they are empowering to the student researchers. Not only do students develop expertise in their chosen areas, they also gain numerous communication skills while deepening their areas of strength. Following each presentation, classmates compliment and then critique the research and demonstration. My students learn how to give and receive constructive feedback.

All project presentations are videotaped. At the end of the year, each student receives a videotape of that year's projects. The tapes reveal student growth over time, typically showing improvement in research strategies, content knowledge, and communication skills.

Although I encourage my students to select their own project topics, I will at times collaborate with them to decide what might be most appropriate to pursue. If I am playing an active role in identifying topics, I try to provide several options so that students learn to make choices. In addition, I require that the students always determine how they will communicate what they have learned to their classmates and myself.

Once the topics are chosen, students complete contracts such as the one shown below. The contract helps organize student work by asking them to identify the steps they will take to complete their work.

Since students are not necessarily self-directed by nature, there are many things a teacher needs to do to help them develop independent learning skills. At the beginning of the school year, I explain that one of the things they will learn is how to conduct independent projects. I tell them that there are "warm-ups" to prepare for this type of learning. These consist of 1) identifying exciting topics, 2) figuring out how and where to get information, and 3) determining how to demonstrate one's learning. We discuss these three warm-ups as a whole class and brainstorm possibilities:

Warming-up to Self-directed Learning:

1. **Identify exciting topics:**

   It's important to ask students what they most want to know. While some initially may not be able to think of anything, most students quickly identify possibilities. Students in the past have suggested whales, computers, molecules, mysteries, famous women, paper making, the Roman Empire, film-making, paradoxes, and the human brain. Sometimes just listening to the enthusiasm of their classmates, encourages others to consider options, however, some students will need teacher assistance in selecting topics.

2. **Figure out where and how to get information:**

   While many topics are fascinating, I suggest that students select ones that are easily researchable. We also discuss different ways to access information. Some students rely on book research, write organizations for printed matter, interview knowledgeable adults, invite guest speakers into the classroom, scan newspapers, watch films or television programs, use telecommunications and appropriate software, or make observations or experiments. Students quickly learn that the process of research can be enjoyable.

3. **Determine how to demonstrate one's learning:**

   Each student is responsible for teaching the rest of the class what he or she has learned. I require that students give project presentations multimodally. Many such demonstrations of learning include charts, videotapes, skits, songs, "talk shows," drawings, dances, slogans, banners, models, dioramas, sculptures, letters, statistics, quilts, community service efforts, and inventions.

After discussing the above three "warm ups", I explain the eight steps of doing a project. I hand out photocopies of the following and we review them as a group.

Eight Steps For Doing Projects

1.   State your goal.
     "I want to understand how visual illusions work."

2.   Put your goal into the form of a question.
     "What are visual illusions and how do they fool our eyes?"

3.   List at least three sources of information you will use.
     Library books on visual illusions
     Eye doctors or university professors
     Prints of M.C. Escher's work
     The art teacher

4.   Describe the steps you will use to achieve your goal.
     Ask the librarian to find books on visual illusions.
     Read those books.
     Look up visual illusion in the encyclopedia and read what it says.
     Talk to the art teacher and maybe others about visual illusions.
     Look at Escher's work.

5.   List at least five main concepts or ideas you want to research.
     What are visual illusions?
     How is the human eye tricked?
     How are they made?
     Who are some artists who have made visual illusion art?
     Can I learn to make some visual illusions?

6.   List at least three methods you will use to present your project.
     Explain what optical illusions are.
     Make a diagram of how the human eye works.
     Make posters with famous optical illusions.
     Try to make optical illusions of my own.
     Hand out a sheet of optical illusions for class members to keep.
     Have the class try to make some.

7.   Organize the project into a timeline.
 Week 1: *Read sources of information.*
 Week 1: *Interview adults.*
 Week 2: *Look at a variety of optical illusions.*
 Week 2: *Try to make my own optical illusions.*
 Week 2: *Make diagram of eye.*
 Week 2: *Make handouts for class.*
 Week 3: *Practice presentation.*
 Week 3: *Present to class.*

8.   Decide how you will evaluate your project.
 Practice in front of my parents and get their feedback.
 Practice in front of Matt and John and get their feedback.
 Ask class for feedback on my presentation and visuals.
 Fill out self-evaluation form.
 Read teacher's evaluation.
 Analyze videotape.

After the class has discussed the eight steps of doing projects, they are usually ready to write their project contracts. The contracts organize their independent learning and inform me of what students intend to study. I keep the contracts in a file folder on my desk. Because the contracts require that research questions and resources be identified immediately, it becomes evident within a day or so whether a contract is actually doable. Sometimes students have to change their topics and when this happens, they complete new contracts. After the first couple of project efforts, however, students become adept at selecting researchable topics. On the next page, you will find the project contract my students complete:

Project Contract

Name: _____   Topic: _____

Research question: _____
_____

List the steps you will take to do this project:

_____
_____
_____
_____

List at least three sources of information you will use:

_____
_____
_____
_____

List at least five concepts you will research:

_____
_____
_____
_____
_____
_____

List at least three ways you will demonstrate what you have learned:

_____
_____
_____
_____

Target completion date:

_____

I have also included the evaluation form I use to assess project work. You will note that the form includes three sections: the first is my written evaluation, the second is where I copy the positive and critical feedback classmates orally provide, and the third section asks the student to assess his or her work.

PROJECT EVALUATION

Teacher Comments:

Research: _____

Information: _____

Organization: _____

Presentation: _____

Other: _____

Peer Comments:

_____

_____

_____

Self-assessment:

What did you learn about your topic? _____

What did you learn about presenting? _____

What was the hardest part for you? _____

What was the best part for you? _____

What do you want to learn more about? _____

MI Homework

In some communities, parents and students expect homework to be assigned on a regular basis even in the primary grades. As a teacher, I attempt to make homework interesting and engaging. I hope that my students will <u>want</u> to do their homework! One unique approach I've discovered is to assign students <u>weekly homework in the seven intelligences.</u> Each week an assignment in one intelligence is sent home to be completed before Friday. Over a period of seven weeks, all seven intelligences are covered and a new rotation begins. Sometimes the homework nicely integrates with class content, and at other times, it is independent of our curricular themes.

My students actually look forward to getting their homework each week. Some are excited because this approach lets them be successful with homework at least some of the time. Students also enjoy the variety of activities, and I appreciate how classroom learning extends into the home and community. Some parents have also told me that they have never witnessed such enthusiasm for learning "after hours."

I have listed seven examples of homework assignments that are appropriate for intermediate grade levels and can easily be adapted for other grades. Sometimes, the homework I assign is directly connected to content we are covering in the classroom. Sometimes, it isn't. Instead, I may try to teach students learning skills through homework or give them activities that I know they will enjoy doing outside of class.

The homework samples below are written directly to students and can be photocopied and distributed if desired.

Linguistic Homework:

Collect three news items during the week about the same topic, such as a war in one part of the world, an election, or the rescue of someone in distress. If you do not have a newspaper, write down what the TV or radio news says about the topic for three days. Compare and contrast what information is shared each day and how different sources, if available, talk about the same event. At the end of the week, be prepared to share with a small group what your topic was and how it changed throughout the week.

Logical-Mathematical Homework:

Your job this week is to hunt for bargains. Look in the newspaper, in the advertisers that come in the mail, in catalogs or coupon books, on TV or radio commercials, or in grocery or other stores.

Find at least 20 items that are on sale. List each item with its regular and its sale price. Then list the amount you would save by purchasing it at the sale price. Record this data on a chart with four columns. At the bottom of the chart, total all of the regular prices, all of the bargain prices, and the total amount saved if you were to purchase all 20 (or more) items.

If possible, try to find items that you or your family would actually buy. In this way, you would be helping to save money for your family budget.

For extra credit, calculate the percentage markdown for each item. For example, if the regular price of an item is $10.00 but the sale price is $5.00, the markdown is 50%. After making all of these calculations, figure the percentage markdown on your total savings.

Kinesthetic Homework:

Design and construct a bridge out of toothpicks and white glue which is both strong and light. As you plan and build your bridge, keep in mind how the weight is distributed along the structure. Your bridge should provide maximum support to the area where the weight will be applied. Use as many toothpicks and as much glue as you want. The bridge should be able to span 18 centimeters. It should be no more than 10 centimeters wide and no more than 24 centimeters long.

There must be a bridge deck that a toy truck could use to cross the bridge. The truck is 4 cm. wide and 5 cm. tall. The deck may be at any level of the bridge.

Your goal should be to make the strongest bridge possible. It will be tested for strength in class on Friday. The strongest bridge will win a prize.

Visual-Spatial Homework:

Make a "flip-flop" with eight questions and answers about a topic we have been studying in school.
- Begin with a square sheet of paper about nine inches on each side.
- Fold it in half, then into four square quarters.
- Unfold it to the original square.
- Fold each of the four corners to the center. (Figure 1)

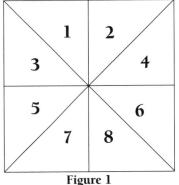

Figure 1

- Turn it over and fold each of the four new corners to the center.
- Fold it in half with the triangles on the inside.
- Stick your thumbs and index fingers under the four flaps.
- Practice flip-flopping your "flip-flop" so that it opens and closes. (Figure 2)
- Now write eight questions or challenges on the eight inside triangles.
- Write the answers beneath each question in the center triangles.
- On the four outside squares name or color four categories. (Figure 1)
- Decorate as you like.

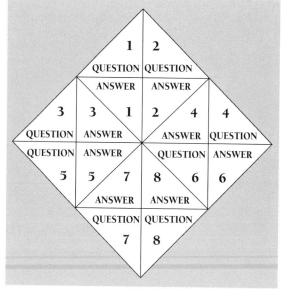

Figure 2

To play, ask a friend to choose a color or category on the outside. Spell that category as you flip-flop to each letter (e.g. p-u-r-p-l-e, opening and closing in opposite directions with each letter). Have your friend choose another number or category and repeat your spelling/counting process. Have your friend choose a third number or category, open to the inside, and read the question on that triangle.

Musical Homework:

Create a rhythm with your hands and feet to teach the class. It can be any combination of clapping hands, stamping feet, patting legs, and snapping fingers. You may also wish to include a short phrase, word, or other vocal sound.

When you present it to the class, you will teach us each part and we will echo your sounds and movements. For example:

Clap, clap, clap
echo
Pat, pat, pat
echo
Clap, clap, pat, pat, snap, snap, snap, "Hey!"
echo

Interpersonal Homework:

This week your homework is to conduct a mini-survey. You need to interview at least ten people and ask them one of the following questions or one of your own. None of your ten people can be from our class, and at least half of them must be adults. Make some kind of chart or graph to show the results of your survey.

Possible questions:
1. At what age do you think students should decide their own bed-times? Why did you suggest that age?
2. Do you think there should be year-round schooling with four or five short breaks? Why or why not?
3. What do you think are the most important things a student should learn at school?
4. Do you think all students should learn to speak another language in grade school? Why or why not?
5. What was your attitude towards school when you were my age?
6. At what age do you think students should be allowed to get jobs?

If you don't like these questions, create ones of your own, however, get your teacher's permission before conducting your mini-survey.

After you get your results:
1. Make a chart or graph to show your results, and
2. Write two conclusions or generalizations you can make from your data.

Intrapersonal Homework:

Make a collage of "you." Begin with a picture of yourself in the center and then surround it with things that characterize you. Use pictures cut out from newspapers, magazines, drawings, clip-art, words, poems, or food labels. Include things like your favorite foods, places, sports, animals, activities, or people.

You can find interesting things to cut out in the movie section of the newspaper, the comics, and the headlines. If you do not have any old magazines or newspapers, ask your neighbors if they have any, or peek into a paper recycling bin. Sometimes libraries have magazines they are discarding.

If you use photographs or magazines, obtain permission from the owner before you cut or paste them. If you decide to glue a three-dimensional object onto your collage, make sure the object is not damaged by glue. If you don't want anyone else to see your collage, get a note from a parent stating that you made one. If you don't mind sharing, we will hang the collages in the classroom on Friday and spend some time looking at our collage gallery.

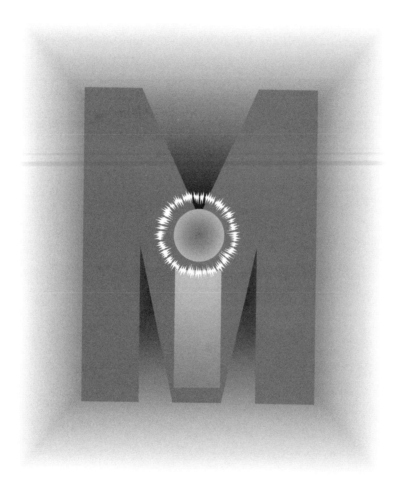

PART VII:
TEACHING MI CURRICULUM UNITS

This section provides teachers with ideas for thematic curriculum units. Complete Multiple Intelligences lessons are not included; instead, I have suggested broad topics that may span several weeks or months. Each year in my classroom I typically cover six to eight units. I integrate the discrete disciplines into my units as well as important district and state goals. Although I suggest timeframes for the curriculum units, they are arbitrary and can be adapted to meet the needs of individual classrooms.

Where do my themes come from? Each summer I like to identify a new theme or two to plan for the coming school year. At the start of school in the fall, I ask my students what they most want to study and together we identify areas that are of interest to them. I also take into account my district's curricular scope and sequence as well as units I have done in the past. From these various sources of input, my six to eight yearly units emerge. Sometimes, when I am more organized than usual, I package up a thematic unit for easy use another time or for sharing with my colleagues. I take a small box and place my lesson plans and needed resources inside. These theme "kits" then are easy to store and share.

Part VII Contents

A List of Theme Possibilities
A Curricular Outline or Mindmap
A Thematic Unit on Discovery
Year Long Thematic Plans:
    Our Only Earth
    Art Around the World
    From Quarks to Quasars
A Thematic Planning Matrix

A List of Theme Possibilities

Sometimes it is helpful to have a list of possible curricular themes. I like to select a single word and see what complexities and extensions it yields for a possible theme. Sometimes I like to take a key word and turn it into a question that guides a curricular unit. For example, the following list includes Technological Inventions as a possible theme. I might transform these key words into a question such as "How has technology both helped and hindered humanity?"

Once I've identified a topic, my next step is to outline or mindmap my potential unit and then break it down into Multiple Intelligences lesson plans. You'll see the curricular development process I go through on the next couple of pages with the theme of "Discovery".

A List of Possible Themes

Discovery
Voyages of discovery
Land journeys of discovery
Flights of discovery
Discovery in space
Microscopic discovery
Subatomic discovery
Possible future discoveries
Personal discovery

Inventions
Architectural inventions
Mechanical inventions
Electrical inventions
Technological inventions
Industrial inventions
Artistic inventions
Medical inventions
Social inventions
Personal inventions

Challenges
Challenges in science
Challenges in the arts

Challenges in
 interpersonal relations
Personal challenges

Changes
Changes in the earth
Changes in nature
Changes in the weather
Changes in cultures
Changes in our bodies
Changes in our families
Changes in our friends
Personal changes

Interdependence
In nature
In communities
Among individuals
Between countries

Democracy
In history
In our country
In other countries
In schools

A CURRICULAR OUTLINE OR MINDMAP

After I identify a particular theme, I next mindmap or outline the main sub-topics I might address into units of study. I also consider important skills for students to acquire during that unit.

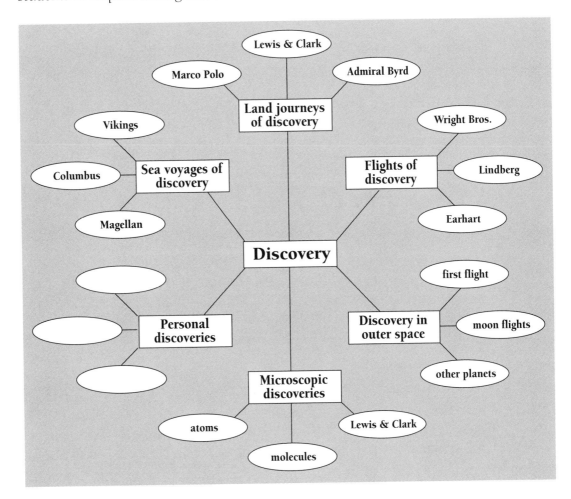

Learning skills to address during the discovery unit:
peer feedback skills
thinking skills: compare and contrast, analyze
historical research skills
self-reflection skills

Possible MI Lessons for Thematic Unit on Discovery

Sea Voyages of Discovery

Vikings:

Linguistic Activity:	Identify and read at least three sources of information on Vikings.
Logical-Mathematical:	Calculate distances they traveled.
Kinesthetic Activity:	Build model Viking ships.
Visual-Spatial Activity:	Illustrate Viking routes on a map.
Musical Activity:	Compose a rhythmic rowing tune.
Interpersonal Activity:	Devise a chain of command on a Viking ship.
Intrapersonal Activity:	Specify the role on a ship one might prefer to assume.

Columbus:

Linguistic Activity:	Read and discuss different perspectives on Columbus.
Logical-Mathematical:	Calculate distance problems: rate x time.
Kinesthetic Activity:	Dramatize his arrival in the Bahamas.
Visual-Spatial Activity:	Make a map of Columbus's voyage.
Musical Activity:	Compare fifteenth- and sixteenth- century music.
Interpersonal Activity:	Make plan for peacefully blending cultures.
Intrapersonal Activity:	Specify how to treat Arawaks and why.

Magellan:

Linguistic Activity:	Write a speech to a king or queen requesting ships for a long trip.
Logical-Mathematical:	Calculate amounts of food, water for trip.
Kinesthetic Activity:	Climb ropes (to trim sails).
Visual-Spatial Activity:	Draw ships, clothing, or other items from that time frame.
Musical Activity:	Learn sea chanties.
Interpersonal Activity:	Role play the ship's return to Spain.
Intrapersonal Activity:	Maintain a captain's log.

Land Journeys of Discovery

Marco Polo

Linguistic Activity: Read and compare historical accounts of
                                voyages.

Logical-Mathematical: Calculate miles per day, week, month, year.
Kinesthetic Activity: Make a board game of his journey.
Visual-Spatial Activity: Draw a scene from one of the countries he
                                visited.

Musical Activity: Compare Chinese and Italian music of the
                                period.

Interpersonal Activity: Contrast Chinese and Italian cultures of the
                                period in small groups.

Intrapersonal Activity: Simulate one of Marco Polo's diary entries.

Lewis and Clark

Linguistic Activity: Read script of Lewis and Clark play.
Logical-Mathematical: Divide script, assign roles and tasks.
Kinesthetic Activity: Construct a set for play.
Visual-Spatial Activity: Make costumes for the play.
Musical Activity: Make simple drums to use for musical
                                accompaniment for the play.

Interpersonal Activity: Re-enact the journey to the Pacific.
Intrapersonal Activity: Reflect on one's role in the play.

Admiral Byrd

Linguistic Activity: Read selections from books such as Byrd's
                                Alone about polar exploration and identify
                                the most important things learned from
                                these voyages.

Logical-Mathematical: Describe the scientific studies accomplished
                                on his voyages.

Kinesthetic Activity: Build a contour map of either pole.
Visual-Spatial Activity: Draw geographic features of either pole.
Musical Activity: Create lyrics for a song about a polar journey.
Interpersonal Activity: Teach one another information learned from
                                Byrd's polar research studies.

Intrapersonal Activity: Describe how one would respond to living
                                alone in a polar environment.

Flights of Discovery

The Wright Brothers

Linguistic Activity: Research lives of the Wright brothers.
Logical-Mathematical: Calculate scale of their planes; compare it with others.
Kinesthetic Activity: Build popsicle stick model planes.
Visual-Spatial Activity: Draw replicas of their planes.
Musical Activity: Learn "Wild, Blue Yonder" song.
Interpersonal Activity: Conduct mock interview with the Wright brothers.
Intrapersonal Activity: Describe whether one would be willing to pioneer
                               such a technological invention.

Charles Lindbergh

Linguistic Activity: Prepare a brief talk on his historic flight or other
                               aspects of his life.
Logical-Mathematical: Compare time, distance with those of other explorers.
Kinesthetic Activity: Lindbergh helped invent new forms of airplanes,
                               missiles, satellites, and artificialhearts.
                               Create a mock invention that represents a
                               new technology.
Visual-Spatial Activity: Look at and draw aerial view of school, community.
Musical Activity: Put together a musical collage that represents
                               different events in Lindbergh's life.
Interpersonal Activity: Discuss different events in his life and their impact
                               on others such as the Lindbergh kidnapping
                               and law, serving as Good Will Ambassador,
                               and mapping airline routes with his wife
                               Anne Morrow.
Intrapersonal Activity: Write: what I would do alone for 34 hours.

Amelia Earhart

Linguistic Activity: Read Earhart's book and cite your favorite passage.
Logical-Mathematical: Compare her plans with Magellan's.
Kinesthetic Activity: Create a series of exercises you might do if
                               seated in one position for long time.
Visual-Spatial Activity: Work with flight simulation software.
Musical Activity: Create a song about her feats and her later
                               disappearance.
Interpersonal Activity: Identify the qualities that caused her to a be a pioneer.
Intrapersonal Activity: In a mode of your choice, explain why she is an
                               inspirational figure.

154

Discoveries in Space

The First Space Flights

Linguistic Activity: Research and teach others about early
                                  space flights.

Logical-Mathematical: Compare dimensions of spacecraft with
                                  planes.

Kinesthetic Activity: Build clay or plaster replicas of spacecraft.
Visual-Spatial Activity: Make a chart of all manned space flights.
Musical Activity: Select music for a flight to space.
Interpersonal Activity: Identify the contributions made by various
                                  countries in early space flights.

Intrapersonal Activity: List 10 things to take into outer space and
                                  explain why you would take them.

The First Lunar Orbits

Linguistic Activity: Create a newscast of the first landing on
                                  the moon. Include Armstrong's speech.

Logical-Mathematical: Calculate speed, distance to lunar orbit.
Kinesthetic Activity: Pantomime moon walking with low gravity.
Visual-Spatial Activity: Diagram booster, spacecraft, lunar lander.
Musical Activity: Create background music for newscast of
                                  first landing on the moon.
Interpersonal Activity: Plan activities for 2 to 3 on a small craft.
Intrapersonal Activity: Identify personal strengths for a long space
                                  trip.

Discoveries Beyond the Solar System

Linguistic Activity: Create a list of recent discoveries in
                                  outer space.

Logical-Mathematical: Create analogies for large distances.
Kinesthetic Activity: Dance or role-play shapes of various
                                  galaxies.

Visual-Spatial Activity: Make computer graphics of space discoveries.
Musical Activity: Simulate outer space sounds (e.g. big bang).
Interpersonal Activity: Study in small interest groups wormholes,
                                  supertwisters, or black holes.

Intrapersonal Activity: Write about inner and outer space.

155

Microscopic Discoveries

Cells

Linguistic Activity: Read Madeline L'Engle's *A Wind in the Door* and discuss its scientific accuracy.

Logical-Mathematical: Calculate rates of cells dividing.

Kinesthetic Activity: Study cells under microscopes.

Visual-Spatial Activity: Watch a videotape or film about microscopic life.

Musical Activity: Note the sound effects or music used in the video or film to reinforce information.

Interpersonal Activity: Study groups on different cell discoveries.

Intrapersonal Activity: Mentally visualize cells dividing in your body.

Molecules

Linguistic Activity: Read fact sheet on molecular discoveries.

Logical-Mathematical: Extrapolate ratios of atoms in molecules.

Kinesthetic Activity: Visit a local science museum that includes information on molecules or molecular discoveries.

Visual-Spatial Activity: Study and draw pictures of DNA double helix.

Musical Activity: Improvise music that resembles molecular structures.

Interpersonal Activity: Compare molecular and human bonding.

Intrapersonal Activity: Each student studies molecules of one element.

Atoms

Linguistic Activity: Provide lecture on atomic discoveries.

Logical-Mathematical: Study Periodic Table of the Elements.

Kinesthetic Activity: Build models of atoms with balls, etc.

Visual-Spatial Activity: Diagram parts of atoms.

Musical Activity: Compose song about parts of an atom.

Interpersonal Activity: Invite a local guest speaker who is a scientist.

Intrapersonal Activity: Choose "favorite" element to study and explain how it is similar to yourself.

Personal Discoveries

Linguistic Activity:	Write about a personal discovery.
Logical-Mathematical:	Create a timeline of personal discoveries.
Kinesthetic Activity:	Dramatize or dance a personal discovery.
Visual-Spatial Activity:	Make a collage of personal discoveries.
Musical Activity:	Identify and share songs that address personal discoveries.
Interpersonal Activity:	Share personal discoveries in small groups.
Intrapersonal Activity:	Set personal goals for future discoveries.

To teach the Discovery unit or any other, teachers will want to determine sequences, complete each lesson plan, and identify and gather resources, as demonstrated in the lesson plans described earlier in the book.

Year Long Thematic Plans

Whenever I do workshops, teachers are often curious about what curriculum units I find enjoyable to teach and my students find enjoyable to study. I have included skeletal outlines of three of my favorite units: From Quarks to Quasars, Art Around the World, and Our Only Earth. While the three units are represented as year-long, in actuality, the time-frame is flexible. These units have been taught in one form or another not only in my intermediate grade classroom but also in primary grades and in middle schools. Certainly all of them could be adapted for high school, just as they have been adapted for other grade levels.

Sample Thematic Unit Plan: "From Quarks to Quasars"

The following curriculum unit is divided into three sections: the microcosm, the human world, and the macrocosm. It integrates common disciplines: language arts, math, science, social studies, health, art, P.E., and music. It is arranged sequentially but could be taught in reverse order: from macrocosm to microcosm. The short film "Powers of Ten" (available on video in most public libraries) is an outstanding way to both open and close the unit.

September : The Microcosm   2-3 weeks

Discipline: Science
- Subatomic particles [2-3 days]
  quarks, leptons, mesons, etc.
- Atoms [1 week]
  elements, the periodic table
- Molecules [1 week]
  compounds, molecular bonding
- Cells [1 week]
  plant and animal cells, cell division

October-April : The Human World   5-7 months

Disciplines: Health, Social Studies, Language Arts
- The human body [2 weeks]
  the brain, the systems
- Human history [2 months]
  prehistory through modern times
- Human accomplishments [2 months]
  discoveries, inventions, creations
- Human cultures [2 months]
  cultures around the world
- Geography of Earth [2-3 weeks]
  continents, mountains, rivers, etc.

May-June : The Macrocosm   4-6 weeks

Disciplines: Science, Social Studies, Language Arts
- The solar system [1 week]
  planets, asteroids, meteors, etc.
- The Milky Way Galaxy [1 week]
  stars and constellations
- The universe [1 week]
  galaxies, black holes, quasars
- Futuristics [1 week]
  cybernetics, technology, what lies ahead?

Sample Thematic Unit Plan: "Art Around the World"

This thematic unit emphasizes social studies and art, but also includes many language arts, math, science, and music activities. There is no necessary sequence; two possibilities are a geographical sequence or an historical sequence. A combination of the two is used below.

Ancient art (September)
Cave paintings, ancient sculpture
Sample activity: making cave-like paintings on brown paper from grocery bags

Art of early civilizations (October)
Sumeria, Egypt, China, India
Sample activity: building pyramids or ziggurats

Greek and Roman art (November)
Sculpture, Architecture, Design
Sample activity: doing clay sculpture

African art (December)
West Africa, South Africa, Central Africa, East Africa
Sample activity: making Adinkra quilt (see *Art from Many Hands* in index)

Asian art (January)
China, Japan, Southeast Asia, India
Sample activity: paper making & block printing

European art (February)
The Renaissance, Impressionism
Sample activity: acrylic painting, water color painting

South and Central American art (March)
Mexico, Guatemala, Peru, Bolivia, Brazil
Sample activity: making sand paintings, yarn art

North American art (April)
Native American art, Colonial arts and crafts, Western art,
Sample activity: toy making, e.g. tops

Modern and contemporary art (May)
Abstract, Expressionistic, new kinds of art
Sample activity: doing collage, bead work, glass, sculpture

Sample Thematic Unit Plan: "Our Only Earth"

Our Only Earth is an interdisciplinary unit that addresses local and global challenges. There is no predetermined order to the following units, nor would it be necessary to teach every section. Teachers might pick and choose topics that are of the greatest interest to their classes. The order suggested below is random; however, in studying these areas most classes find that they are interdependent and overlap in many ways.

September 15 - October 31:
Our Troubled Skies
Air pollution, global warming, the ozone layer

November 1- December 15:
The Ocean Crisis
Water pollution, whaling, land erosion and runoff

January:
Tropical Rain Forests
Deforestation, land degradation, extinction

February:
Endangered Species
Vanishing plants and animals

March:
The Energy Crisis
Problems with production; alternative sources

April:
War, The Global Battlefield
Human conflicts around the world

May:
Our Divided World
Overpopulation, poverty, and hunger

At the conclusion of each topic, a problem-solving process should be undertaken to enable students to suggest and perhaps even implement their solutions. A variety of community service projects often emerge.

An excellent set of resources for this unit is the "Our Only Earth" series of classroom manuals for global problem-solving available through Zephyr Press, Tucson, Arizona.

Teachers often want a visual format to guide the development of their curricular plans. Two different formats follow: The first specifies MI activities while the second highlights the major conceptual areas curriculum will address. Many teachers like to enlarge the following charts to make it easier to include as much information as possible.

A Thematic Planning Matrix

Theme Focus_____ Unit _____

Grade Level _____ Time frame: _____

Key Topics or Questions:

Desired Outcomes:	Linguistic Activities	Logical-Mathematic	Kinesthetic Activities	Visual-Spatial	Musical Activities	Inter-personal	Intra-personal	Materials
Assesment Activities:								
Culminating Activities:								

THEMATIC PLANNING FORM

Theme: _____

Sequence of units: 1._____
                              2._____
                              3._____
                              4._____

Unit 1 subtopics:
                    1._____
                    2._____   Lessons{
                    3._____

Unit 1 assessment: _____

Unit 2 subtopics:
                    1._____
                    2._____   Lessons{
                    3._____

Unit 2 assessment: _____

Unit 3 subtopics:
                    1._____
                    2._____   Lessons{
                    3._____

Unit 3 assessment: _____

Unit 4 subtopics:
                    1._____
                    2._____   Lessons{
                    3._____

Unit 4 assessment: _____

Overall assessment: _____

A FINAL WORD

Throughout this book, I have tried to share some of the ways I adapt the Theory of Multiple Intelligences to my classroom. I think as teachers, however, it is important to develop approaches that work best for you, for your students, and your community.

In looking back over my years of teaching with this model, I wanted to share a few reflections. I have been willing to do extra planning and create new assessment processes because of the way my students have responded and because of the success I have experienced as a professional. I'd like to explain some of the tangible results I have achieved that motivate me to continue.

What are some of the results of this program?

I have conducted action research projects in my classroom to assess what effects if any this classroom model has on intermediate-aged students. To do the research, I maintained a daily journal with specific entries that recorded the following:

general daily reflections

daily evaluation of how focused or "on-task" students were

evaluation of transitions between centers

explanation of any discipline problems

self-assessment — how my teacher-time was used

tracking of specific individuals, previously identified as students with serious behavior problems

In addition, I administered a "Classroom Climate Survey" twelve times during the year, a "Student Assessment Inventory" of the Multiple Intelligences learning centers nine times, and a "Center's Group Survey" eight times during the year.

The data I gathered revealed the following:

1. Students develop increased responsibility, self-direction, and independence over the course of the year. Although I have not attempted to compare my students with those in other classes, the self-direction and motivation they exhibit has been consistently apparent to literally hundreds of classroom visitors. The students become skilled at developing their own projects, gathering necessary resources and materials, and making well-planned presentations.

2. Discipline problems significantly reduce. Students previously identified as having serious behavior problems show rapid improvement in social skills typically during the first six weeks of school. By mid-year, they are often making important contributions to their groups. And by year's end, they occasionally assume positive leadership roles at the centers.

3. All students develop and apply new skills. In the fall, most students typically describe only one center as their favorite. (Interestingly enough, the distribution among the seven centers is always relatively even.) By mid-year, most identify three to four favorite centers. By year's end, nearly every student identifies at least six centers as favorites. Moreover, they all make multimodal presentations of their independent projects which include songs, skits, visuals, poems, games, surveys, puzzles, and group participation activities, the skills they are developing at the seven centers.

4. Cooperative learning skills improve in all students. Since so much of the center work is collaborative, students become highly skilled at listening, helping each other, sharing leadership in different activities, accommodating group changes, and introducing new classmates to the program. They learn not only to respect each other but also to appreciate and call upon the unique gifts and abilities of their classmates.

5. Academic achievement has improved as measured by both classroom and standardized tests. CAT scores are at or above local, state and national averages in all areas. Retention is high on classroom year-end tests. Methods for recalling information are predominately musical, visual, and kinesthetic, indicating the influence of working through the different intelligences. I have observed students who were previously unsuccessful in school become high-achievers in new areas.

In summary, it is clear that students' learning improves. Many students say they enjoy school for the first time. As the school year progresses, new skills emerge. Some students discover musical abilities, artistic, literary, mathematical, and other capacities. Some become skilled leaders. In addition, self confidence and motivation increase significantly. Finally, students develop responsibility, self-reliance and independence as they take an active role in shaping their own learning experiences.

What is the teacher's role in a Multiple Intelligence program?

One interesting consequence of a student-centered classroom such as this is the role of the teacher. While the majority of students are at work in the centers and on projects, my time is spent with individuals or small groups. I help students learn new skills, tutor those with reading or math difficulties, assist gifted students with challenging activities, and work with small groups to design structures, create dances, and plan projects. Additionally, I often confer with individual students, evaluating their work, suggesting opportunities for improvement, and giving positive feedback. So, my role has become that of facilitator, guide, and resource provider. My relationships with students are more personal and I am gratified by their individual accomplishments.

Not only has my role changed but I have also developed new competencies as a result of teaching in a such an environment. I have learned to observe my students from multiple perspectives. I have become more accomplished at preparing for diverse methods of learning and gathering resources to facilitate learning that is center- and project-based. I also find that I am working with my students, rather than for them, exploring what they explore, discovering what they discover, and often learning what they learn. My satisfaction is gleaned from my students' enthusiasm for learning and their independence, rather than from their test scores and ability to sit quietly Perhaps most importantly, because of planning for such diverse modes of learning, I have become more creative and multimodal in my own thinking and learning. I sometimes wonder who is changing the most; the students or myself?

Why is a Multiple Intelligences model successful?

The program has been successful not only in my classroom but in hundreds more around the country where it has been adopted. There seem to be two reasons for the success. First, every student has an opportunity to specialize and excel in at least one area of human intelligence. Usually, however, it is three or four. Since I began this program, there has not been a single student unable to find an area of specialty and success. Second, each student is learning subject matter in multiple ways and has a variety of opportunities to understand and retain academic information. Moreover, because of the input students have into the program, their learning experiences are personally meaningful.

Many student needs are met through this program. Their intellectual needs are met through the constant challenges in their daily activities. Emotional needs are met at times by working closely with others and at other times by working independently. Ultimately, I believe that students working in an MI environment develop new strengths and come to better understand and appreciate themselves as individuals. Because of the skills the students develop, they have multiple abilities to pursue their interests long after they leave my classroom. And that has always been my goal as an educator: to inspire a love of learning in each child I teach.

Multiple Intelligences Reference List

Books:

Armstrong, Thomas. *In Their Own Way*, Los Angeles: Tarcher, 1987.

Benzie, Teresa. *A Moving Experience: Dance for Lovers of Children and the Child Within.* Tucson: Zephyr Press, 1987.

Blood-Patterson, Peter. *Rise Up Singing*. Bethlehem, PA: Sing Out Corporation, 1988.

Brookes, Mona. *Monart: Drawing with Children*. Los Angeles: Tarcher, 1986.

Burns, Marilyn. *A Collection of Math Lessons, Books 1-3*. White Plains, NY: Math Solutions Publications, Cuisenaire Co. of America, 1987.

Campbell, Linda et al. *Teaching & Learning through Multiple Intelligences.* Needham Heights, MA: Allyn & Bacon, 1994.

Campbell, Linda, McKisson, Micki, Campbell, Bruce. *Our Only Earth: A Global Problem-Solving Series*. Tucson, AZ: Zephyr Press, 1990.

Csikszentmihalyi, Mihaly. *Flow: The Psychology of Optimal Experience*. New York: Cambridge University Press, 1990.

Dickinson, Dee. *Creating the Future: Perspectives on Educational Change.* Seattle: New Horizons for Learning, 1990.

Drew, Nancy. *Learning the Skills of Peacemaking*. Rolling Hills Estates, CA: Jalmar Press, 1987.

Dunn, Rita and Dunn, Kenneth. *Teaching Students through Their Individual Learning Styles: A Practical Approach*. Reston, VA: Prentice Hall, 1978.

Educational Testing Service and Harvard Project Zero. *Arts Propel: An Introductory Handbook*. Harvard Graduate School of Education: Cambridge, 1991.

Galyean, Beverly. *Mindsight: Learning through Imaging.* Zephyr Press, Tucson, 1988.

Gardner, Howard. *Frames of Mind: The Theory of Multiple Intelligences.* NY: Basic Books, 1983.

Gardner, Howard. *Multiple Intelligences: The Theory in Practice.* NY: Basic Books, 1993.

Gilbert, Anne. *Teaching the Three R's through Movement.* NY: MacMillan, 1989.

Gilbert, Anne. *Creative Dance for All Ages.* Reston, VA: American Alliance for Health, Physical Education, Recreation and Dance, 1992.

Koch, Kenneth and Farrell, Kate. *Talking to the Sun.* New York: Henry Holt, 1985.

Koch, Kenneth. *Wishes, Lies, and Dreams: Teaching Poetry to Children.* New York: Henry Holt, 1979.

Lewis, Barbara. *The Kids Guide to Social Action.* Minneapolis, MN: Free Spirit Publishing, 1991.

Liem, Tik. *Invitations to Science Inquiry.* Chino Hills, CA: Science Inquiry Enterprises, 1981.

MacMillan *Visual Dictionary.* New York: MacMillan, 1992.

Ruef, Kerry. *The Private Eye: (5X) Looking/Thinking by Analogy.* Seattle, WA: The Private Eye Project, 1992.

Samples, Bob. *Open Mind, Whole Mind.* Rolling Hills Estate, CA: Jalmar Press, 1987.

Schuman, Jo. *Art from Many Hands: Multicultural Art Projects.* Worcester, MA: Davis Publications, 1981.

Wiseman, Ann. *Making Things, Books 1 & 2.* Boston: Little, Brown & Co, 1974.

Articles:

Campbell, Bruce. "Multiple Intelligences in the Classroom." In Context
  Quarterly. No. 27. Winter, 1991.

Campbell, Bruce. "Multiple Intelligences in Action." Childhood Education.
  Summer, 1992.

Krechevsky, Mara. "Project Spectrum: An Innovative Assessment Approach."
  Educational Leadership. Vol. 48. No. 5, Feb. 1991.

Seidel, Steve. "Collaborative Assessment Conferences. . ." Project Zero: Harvard
  Graduate School of Education, Cambridge, MA., 1991.